My Happiness Button

Your Down-to-Earth Guide to a Happy Life

Felix New

A CIP catalogue record for this title is available from the British Library.

ISBN Paperback: 978-1-9160294-0-8
ISBN E-book: 978-1-9160294-1-5

First printed 2019

To everybody who believes in me.
Your support means everything.

CONTENTS

INTRODUCTION

Thank you for picking up this book and congratulations on investing in your happiness. The discoveries and practices I present to you have truly transformed my life and have allowed me to become, as lame as it may sound, 'a happy person'.

I'm sure that the knowledge you'll gain from this book will also transform your life. *My Happiness Button* is a down-to-earth guide for everyone to achieve true and lasting happiness.

I want to address two burning questions you might have:

1. There are 100's of books on happiness out there, what's so different about this one?

2. What on earth is a 'Happiness Button'?

Question 1: What's different about this book?

You may have picked up this book thinking, *"Hey, maybe I can be happy with the push of a button, that would be cool!"*

No book is the same when it's written from the heart and reflects a person's life experience. For instance, there is only one Felix New with his own unique take on happiness.

I find that many self-help books on happiness treat the issue of 'developing happiness' as an extremely vague concept. Readers are often left with the following takeaway: "Okay, author X says I should be more of X, I guess I'll do a little more of that somehow."

In *My Happiness Button*, we don't tolerate vagueness. We break each step down until it's clear how to achieve and apply happiness to our lives. Before we dive into the steps to developing happiness, we first start by clearly defining it and debunking myths around the topic. This will ensure we're all on the same page!

Question 2: What on earth is a Happiness Button?

A Happiness Button is the collection of steps you take and realisations you have that will increase your happiness. Although it may be weak at times, you already have a Happiness Button within you. It shows up on birthdays, when your favourite team wins with a smashing victory, after a success at work or during unexpected kindness from a stranger. It's time to stop leaving your happiness up to chance!

As you read this book, you'll learn seven essential skills that I have found to be fundamental building blocks of a happy life. While applying these steps, you'll become aware of a 'happiness force' within you. This force is your Happiness Button at work. I like to call it 'a force of happiness production'.

This book will act as your clear guide in developing the different aspects of your Happiness Button, understanding the basic concepts behind them, and learning how to effectively use them to increase happiness in your life.

You may have picked up this book thinking, *"Hey, maybe I can be happy with the push of a button, that would be cool!"* However, everything worth keeping takes time and effort. Although some steps such as *gratitude* will make you feel happy instantly, developing the skills in this book will take patience. Some may even be a little challenging but well worth it. Working on our happiness is a life-long job, so let's waste no more time in getting started.

MY STORY

Christmas break, December 2012. After my first three months at law school, I arrived at my parents' house with a suitcase full of unwashed clothes, a beard that couldn't remember the last time it saw a trimmer, and some serious bags of fatigue under my eyes. All I could think about was food, TV, sleep - repeat. I had experienced exhaustion countless times before, but something felt different this time. It would stay with me for the next four years to come, never leaving my side.

A visit to the doctor and four (giant) blood samples confirmed what my parents and I suspected - I was diagnosed with glandular fever and a severe liver infection.

"You'll be fine in 3 weeks, just take some rest and eat some greens", the doctor said cheerfully. Oh, how I wished that was true. Three weeks passed, and still no sign of improvement. It took me four years to get back to my normal energy levels. To say the least, this period of my life was a real struggle. Glandular fever, and the post-viral fatigue I would experience pushed me to the edge, and I was holding on with the last grain of my strength. Illness can suck all life out of you, making simple tasks such as going to the grocery store seem like running a marathon and making you question if you're still human or now officially a zombie.

Would you think I'm crazy if I told you I'm glad I got ill? I'm extremely glad. Not because I was able to watch Netflix all day but because the experience of severe illness marked the beginning of finding true happiness.

Looking at the overly familiar four walls of my room, my eyes opened to realisations I never had before. It took being stripped to the basics to find the richness of life. I began to undertake a process of deeply exploring the human mind and the topic of happiness. It was an incredible thirst and this previously unknown information on happiness was the only remedy to quench it.

What followed were countless hours of reflecting on the findings I acquired from a myriad of books, journal articles, YouTube videos, films, conversations with family members, and friends and strangers from all walks of life - ranging from supermarket cashiers in my local area to Buddhist monks in the Japanese mountains of Koyasan. I am so grateful for having discovered and developed this understanding of happiness. Who knows how much longer I would have had to search and live miserably if I didn't have the experience of severe illness as a wake-up call?

American singer and actor, Leif Garret said, *"I've come to understand that there's always something positive, even in a negative situation."* I'm a firm believer in the idea that blessings in disguise are all around us. With

My Happiness Button, I'm sharing the insight and lessons I've learned from my life and engaging with the topic of happiness in a digestible and directly applicable way. This life is damn beautiful, and I want this book to be your wake-up call, without having to go through a severe illness as I did.

Many of these principles and concepts may be as new to you as they once were for me. So, I will start with briefly outlining concepts before showing you straightforward ways to apply them to your life. If there is anything you already know, see it as an opportunity to refresh your knowledge or the potential to discover a new angle. After all, learning from each other's life experience is one of the most valuable resources available to us.

There are seven essential steps to happiness that we will cover in this book. Each of them has its own chapter. I strongly encourage you to give each step the attention it deserves. Allow the benefits of each step to manifest in your life. There is a treat hiding for you in Chapter 10. The chapter is a collection of diverse steps you can take that will also increase your happiness immensely. I call them happiness boosters. The boosters include mostly advice on lifestyle choices for a happy life: what to eat/drink, how to sleep, who to spend time with, and much more! You can think of Chapter 10 as a toolkit to further upgrade and personalise your Happiness Button.

"I've come to understand that there's always something positive, even in a negative situation."

Leif Garret

Before we dive in, I want to truly say **thank you.** Thank you for picking up this book and letting me be part of your life. I'm as excited about your transformation as you hopefully are!

CHAPTER ONE: HAPPINESS EXPLAINED

What on Earth is Happiness?

I know you've felt happy and I know you've felt unhappy. I also know that although you want to be happier, you're sometimes confused about what happiness actually is. How do I know that? Because you're human. Before diving into the research that would result in this book, I was in the dark about happiness too, yet had a deep longing for a happier life.

If I try to recall moments of feeling happy, my mind takes me to my childhood. I still remember those feelings of joy. Everything was magical. I felt like I was in a bubble of blissfulness and nothing could bring me

down. I even had a special t-shirt I would only wear on birthdays with a smiling baby giraffe on it. I would feel a sense of joy flowing through my body when I went to the bottom drawer of my wardrobe to put it on, ready to embrace what wonderful things this day would bring. I need to give credit to my mum here; this happiness was mostly due to her amazing baking skills and her intriguing ability to wrap presents. She could wrap a toy car in a way that would make you think it's a football. Crazy stuff.

Before you drift off into thoughts about your childhood birthday parties, let's deal with one critical question.

What on earth is happiness?

Is it even possible to describe happiness? Is there even a need to do so? Can't I simply put on a t-shirt with a smiling baby giraffe on it and feel good?

If I asked you what happiness is right now, you might struggle to give me a confident answer. We rarely have discussions with our friends, family, teachers or colleagues about what happiness means. Instead, we remain in a hazy state, longing for it to come. Maybe I'm being unfair, and you could give me a pretty solid answer!

However, happiness is not a concrete concept and can be defined in many ways. The guy sitting next to you in the café would probably disagree with your idea of happiness and interject with his own definition of it. *'No, that's wrong. Happiness is when I take my refurbished Ford Mustang out for a spin on a Sunday mornin'.*

Part of the struggle is that we use the word *happy* to mean different things in day-to-day life. *I'm happy to meet you...she had a happy childhood...that was a happy coincidence... it's happy hour*! ...are all different versions of happiness. All this haziness makes our job just a little harder.

Is it even possible to describe happiness? Is there even a need to do so? Can't I simply put on a t-shirt with a smiling baby giraffe on it and feel good?

Isn't happiness subjective and different for every single person?

Aren't some people by default just happier than others? Isn't it all just genetics?

Isn't there a difference between long term feelings (I am happy) and short-term feelings (I feel happy about this)?

Surely, you can't compare the guy from the café (and his obsession with his Ford Mustang) with the happiness you get when you finally see an old friend again or during the birth of your first child?

These are all very legitimate questions that people have asked me when discussing happiness. Did I manage to get your brain smoking trying to make sense of happiness? Good! That means you are on the path of moving past all the confusion, and towards a clearer understanding of happiness. Although the exact definition is not so important, we need to become much clearer about happiness if we wish to have more of it in our lives. How could you expect to receive something when you're not even sure what it is?

We often idealise knowledgeable and successful people yet many of them will tell you that the key to success is to assume you know very little. That's the approach I try to take. Even though I have put together this book, I am still a student seeking more understanding every single day. It's my goal to always remain in a knowledge-seeking state as this is how we grow and ensure we don't become stagnant. If our worldview is flexible, we will develop a deeper understanding of life.

What Happiness is Not...

"To pursue a goal which is by definition unattainable is to condemn oneself to a state of perpetual unhappiness"

Émile Durkheim
(Influential Sociologist)

We all want to reduce uncertainty and we all want to achieve our dreams and desires. Why else do we go to work every single day? Most of us get frustrated when our lives don't look as we imagined, especially in comparison to our friends! As a result, the perceived highest state of happiness for many of us is to be in full control of our lives and acquire everything we ever dreamed of having. We believe that this will make all of our problems dissolve.

There is a huge problem with this approach to happiness and it's pretty fundamental. It's **impossible to achieve!** It's impossible because too much of life is out of our control. You will never be able to control the cycle of life. You can have plastic surgery to look like a Hollywood star (I won't mention names). You can eat every superfood on the planet. You can have the best doctors on your side. You will never be able to stop the aging process (not with current science at least). Equally, you are not in control of the choices other people make. You can advise them, you can give them a list of reasons why they should do what you think, you could even intimidate them (please don't) but at the end of the day, other people make their own choices, and sometimes it goes against your idea of happiness.

The same goes for acquiring possessions. If you want to buy a specific dog from the pet shop and the dog dies overnight, there is nothing you can do about it. Sorry for the bleak example but emotions are key to remembering! Equally, we may think we will be happy once we get the car we want but what we *want* changes all the time. It changes so quickly that our bank account will never be able to keep up.

You want what you can't have.

That is how humans work. If you get into the trap of defining your happiness in terms of acquiring everything you can't have, then you will always be working against an unreachable goal. The carrot and stick is a good example. Even if the donkey gets the carrot, he's still a donkey and will soon chase a new carrot on a stick. There will always be a newer, faster and better version of what you desire. There will soon be something else in your life you crave but can't have. A new apartment, a new 4K camera, a more 'attractive' partner – it's a never-ending cycle. If you happen to be so rich that you can afford anything you want, you will become unhappy because there will no longer be anything you can chase for a fix of happiness. You will be sick of carrots.

The desire for acquiring possession hit me especially hard after I dropped out of law school and I took a job in a sports shop for £5 an hour. On my way to work, I would walk past shops with expensive clothes and watches which were unaffordable for a young guy stacking shoes for a living. I thought that when I could finally walk into these shops and buy everything I want, I will be fulfilled. I truly felt the capitalist spirit alive in me. It was one of the only things that kept me going back to work to earn more money. I worked and I saved up. One day, I had enough money to buy a rose-gold watch for £350. I felt like a boss. I was proud to wear it. I would look down at my arm and feel good about myself. No one would assume I worked in a sports shop. After two weeks, I started to get used to the watch. It was no longer so special to me. The novelty had worn off along with the shiny new look the watch once had. It didn't make me feel good anymore. Now it was just another object, just like the spoon I use to stir my food. I had my eyes on some new clothes now. Maybe having a new look would fulfill me longer?

At this time in my life, I had a constant feeling of

lack. I focused on achieving happiness through material means. It was the best I could do to become happy. I wanted to be in control of my life and happiness. You might have experienced a similar feeling in your life. That's why the liberal capitalist system and materialism is successful. You have the *winners* with the flashy items and the *losers* with no money, striving for the flashy items.

If happiness were a pill, it would be the most desired product on the planet. People pay a lot of money and severely damage their bodies in the pursuit of happiness. This way of life and pleasure-seeking is known as *hedonism.*

If this is your approach to happiness, then you won't achieve it. If you're still chasing material things and hoping that being in control of everything in your life will bring you ultimate lasting happiness, this should be your wake-up call, my friend!

Then What is Happiness?

These days, according to psychologists, happiness is often assessed by asking the following question.

Is it possible for a person to maintain a sense of well-being over a longer period of time?

If so, they could be labeled happy. If not, then you might consider them unhappy. This approach allows for ups and downs, but it concentrates on a long-term positive state. Since this approach includes a personal judgement about well-being, the method is subjective and therefore difficult to accurately measure. No one likes to admit to themselves that they are unhappy, even if they are. Why should we call ourselves unhappy? That will make us even more unhappy.

Despite the potential difficulty to construct an accurate measure that genuinely captures how happy a person is, this method takes us away from a theory of happiness where we try to control everything in our lives and continuously chase possessions. Instead, it focuses on the individual and how they might be feeling over a period of time. That makes sense to me, how about you?

To spice things up a little, let's look at a real-life example of someone trying to move closer to lasting happiness. Like many of us, Mo Gawdat (former chief business officer at Google X) found it extremely difficult to figure out what made him happy. Mo worked as a stock trader and tech executive in Dubai, facing depression every single day as his income increased exponentially but his happiness declined drastically. A software engineer by training, he would spend over ten years researching happiness and with the help of his son, applied his mathematical genius to form an algorithm. Mo had no idea how badly he would need this happiness algorithm as his son unexpectedly died at the age of 21. In a recent viral Facebook video, Mo spoke to Channel 4 about his book, *Solve for Happy: Engineer Your Path to Joy* where he describes the happiness formula and how he put it to test. He says, *"Happiness is not about what the world gives you; it is about what you think about what the world gives you."*

Mo argues that happiness is being content and accepting of the life that has presented itself to you. Looking at the glass as half full rather than half empty. He's now left Google with the goal of making one billion people happy. Hats off to that! (onebillionhappy.org)

Mo isn't alone in his understanding of happiness. Relating to the ancient Greek philosophy of *Stoicism*, Epictetus said *"man is disturbed not by things, but by the views he takes of them."* He also said, *"we have two ears and one mouth so that we can listen twice as much as we speak"* but that's a different story.

Although this understanding is great, I would like to propose that there is more to happiness than just being satisfied. Sonya Lyumbomirsky, a best-selling author and professor of psychology says it perfectly when she calls happiness a 'state of mind' - *"a way of perceiving and approaching ourselves and the world in which we reside. So, if you want to be happy tomorrow, the day after, and for the rest of your life, you can do it by choosing to change and manage your state of mind."*

This certainly takes us closer to uncovering the meaning of happiness.

Being Happy vs. Feeling Happy

What then is *being* happy? A depressed person can be happy when something happens that brings them joy but would you call them a happy person in general? You probably wouldn't. Equally, a person who is mostly content, calm and joyful will have moments of sadness, but does that make them an unhappy person? No, it doesn't.

Being happy is something more constant than an event or sudden feeling.

This leads us to my own definition of happiness.

My Definition

"Happiness can be thought of as a <u>state</u> <u>of</u> <u>mind</u>. When one experiences 'positive' emotions considerably more often than 'negative' ones. A happy life is not absent of 'negative' emotions and thoughts. Instead, it is a life where emotions and thoughts are managed effectively, thus leaving a person with an overall positive state of mind a.k.a. Happiness."

Felix New

Positive emotions don't just mean feeling joyful or grinning all day like a hyena. Enthusiasm, engagement, tranquillity, and confidence also constitute positive emotions. Of course, you don't reach these things magically. They need to be developed and worked on. The problem is, we rarely get taught how to develop this state of mind effectively, so go through painful experience after painful experience until we begin to shape our lives more sustainably. Although suffering and pain can be a great teacher, many of us go through a lot of unnecessary suffering.

From this point forward, you will become equipped with a range of tools and realisations that will help you develop this happy state of mind and eliminate unnecessary suffering.

Importantly, developing happiness can relate to biological and socio-economic factors. These do not determine your happiness but they need to be understood and managed. To address the elephant in the room and to dispel a common myth, genetics *do* play a part in determining your state of mind but developing a positive state of mind is a skill you can hone.

How Many 'Positive' Emotions Do We Need?

We don't always need to take an approach to life where we frantically aim to accumulate and strive for more, as people do in the hamster-wheel of the corporate world. We need to become aware of how we're truly feeling and naturally we'll start to insert things into our life that serve us. As a result of this mindful and self-loving approach, we will feel more positive emotions. If you have times of feeling bad, you don't need to hit the alarm button because something seems to have gone wrong. It's important that we face these darker feelings when working towards becoming happier. Let's step out of the race of always wanting to become the best at everything. Simply by being here, you are already doing a fantastic job. You are filling your cup with life and bliss. Remember, you can't serve from an empty cup. You are doing this for yourself but also for everyone you love.

Different Experiences of Happiness

Some key factors can impact your happiness, genetics, environment, culture, and generation are all things that can influence you but should never be used as an excuse for being unhappy.

Your Genetic Make-Up

A heavily debated question is whether we have 'set levels' of happiness or have the capability of 'setting our levels' of happiness?

About a year ago, I was talking to a stranger about writing a book on happiness. He said, "what's the point of writing a book on happiness when we're all just naturally more or less happy according to our genetic make-up. Some of us are threes, and some of us are nines. Isn't that all there is to it?" Unsurprised at this commonly held belief, I replied. "Good sir, I can assure you that we do have a say when it comes to our happiness. It isn't all determined by genetics - I am living proof of it!" Then I went on a rant that left my conversation partner with wide eyes of amazement. He was confronted by the realisation that he went over 60 years of his life without ever thinking it was possible to have a say on how he was feeling. He just accepted his happiness level as determined by his genetics and mind.

So, what should you take from this? What are the facts?

There is some evidence that mood-altering illnesses such as depression can be passed on genetically. In those cases, your happiness level can be influenced by genetics. There is also new evidence that happiness itself might well be genetically passed on. In 2016, one of the largest behavioral genetics studies was published in *Nature Genetics* (nature.com). 190 international researchers analysed the genomes of 298,420 people, looking for 'the happy gene'. The researchers found that there were three genetic varieties for a person's sense of well-being and a genetic component to what they defined as happiness. Although we shouldn't draw too many conclusions from this study just yet, it's certainly an intriguing finding.

Does that mean you're stuck with the genetic 'cards' your body has dealt you?

Not at all, far from it!

In recent years, research and countless self-help books have demonstrated that we certainly have a say in our levels of happiness. We can influence our levels of happiness by utilising happiness boosting techniques such as mindfulness. Also, the findings of the international study published in *Nature Genetics*, point out that the degree of genetic influence on your happiness is still not fully known and that environmental factors are greatly responsible for your levels of happiness. Sonja Lyubomirsky argues in *The How of Happiness: A Scientific Approach to Getting the Life You Want,* that 50% of long-term happiness levels are determined by genetics, 10% by life circumstances and an astonishing 40% is down to self-control and techniques we apply. This 40% can be manipulated and changed positively. One thing is for sure; there are indeed a good degree of non-genetic elements to happiness.

There is now a branch of psychology that focuses on what makes humans happy! It's called 'positive psychology' and a central idea is that you can elevate your happiness in the same way you can learn a new skill. Even if you were dealt difficult genetic cards, you still have a say in your level of happiness, That's excellent news for all of us!

Your Circumstances and Environment

I was always told money doesn't buy you happiness. Although this is true, having money *does* take some stress and strain away from your life. However, research shows that the link between money and happiness only applies until a certain level of income (around $75,000). After that, it will do very little for you. Money simply provides some financial freedom but is not the be all and end all of happiness.

It can be challenging to be happy when you live in depressing or even life-threatening circumstances such as a war, severe illness or an abusive relationship. In such cases, your priority should be survival and improving

Well, Felix, tell me how I'm supposed to be happy when I have a student loan to pay off, I can't pay the bills, I'm depressed about the rain in this stupid country, and I live in an unsafe neighbourhood. How can I be happy when my environment and circumstances suck?

your situation as soon and as much as possible. Many of the steps to happiness should still apply to you even in this difficult time. When I was suffering from severe illness, many of the steps in this book made my days much brighter.

Your circumstances and environment matter for your happiness. Although trying to be in control of everything in life is unattainable, some degree of 'being in control of your destiny' is important for feeling secure and fulfilled. Although economic and societal factors are harder to change, smaller issues can often be changed on a personal and daily level. This might mean leaving an environment altogether if it's possible and necessary.

> *Well, Felix, tell me how I'm supposed to be happy when I have a student loan to pay off, I can't pay the bills, I'm depressed about the rain in this stupid country, and I live in an unsafe neighbourhood. How can I be happy when my environment and circumstances suck?*

The key here is very straightforward, but many of us often find it difficult to put into action.

Change what you can and _accept what you can't_.

If your neighbourhood is unsafe, move somewhere safer (even if that means moving to a smaller flat). If you can't stand the rain, move abroad as soon as you can or learn to stop hating the rain. If you are not earning enough, keep applying for jobs until you achieve what you need. Can you sell things on eBay as a side hustle? Is there truly nothing you can do to increase your income? If you can't pay off your student debt, how is being unhappy about it going to change anything? _Change what you can and accept what can't, right now_. It's the best you can do to deal with life, your circumstances, and your environment effectively. Showing gratitude for what you have is also a game-changer that will work wonders for you (see chapter

5).

What it boils down to is this: Even if you can't control everything in your life, you can always control your response. Chapters 3-10 will give you some valuable gems to guide you.

The Culture You Were Born in

My sister is an anthropologist, so I had to add this section to the book, or she'd be mad at me. Anthropology is the study of human behaviour. Interestingly enough, she's currently doing a Ph.D. on the Anthropology of Happiness (it must run in the family).

Understandings of happiness can differ culturally. The French often value social get-togethers to drink wine and eat frogs and snails (excuse the generalisation). Is that also your idea of happiness? The French surely think it makes them happy. Jokes aside, beware that the culture around you can well be shaping your happiness!

There are key differences between collectivist cultures (Latin America, Asia, Africa) and more individualistic cultures (Europe, U.S). The Kingdom of Tonga is an excellent example of a collectivist culture. On its more than 170 South Pacific islands, people base a lot of their happiness on their social relationships, roles and responsibilities. If people don't have good relationships with their family and friends or don't fulfil social roles, it will be harder for them to be happy. In the western world, the perceived source of happiness is more often based on how you are doing as an individual. Many people find it difficult to be happy if their circumstances are bad, even if they are fulfilling their social roles and responsibilities.

This shows us that happiness is not only based on pre-determined biological factors but also cultural differences. Happiness is a concept we create. This leaves room to re-create happiness for yourself too. Live by your own rules and be aware of the culture around you that may well be shaping how you feel.

Your Generation

Seeking happiness is a relatively modern phenomenon in the West. Until the 18th and 19th centuries, people were living far more miserably, and were less active in seeking happiness. Just think about Oliver Twist! The general public were grumpy and miserable, and wore dark, grubby clothing (again, excuse the generalisation). Life was often depressing and that was okay. It was normal.

Living to be happy is a new trend in history but *oh boy*, has it taken off. Happy meals were introduced in 1979 and thrill-inducing theme parks have been popping up left, right and center. *Happy* by Pharrell Williams, released in 2013, sold millions of copies. Would a song about happiness have taken off in the Middle Ages? Probably not. They preferred sacred songs played on the Psaltery (a cross between harp and lyre).

The source of our happiness has evolved hugely over time. Today it is perfectly acceptable in many societies to stay single for your whole life if you desire. It is also more or less acceptable to download an app and swipe through 100's of profiles until you find someone that you find appealing enough to spend an evening with. Such ideas of transient intimacy would have been unthinkable when your great-grandparents were alive. If they were single, they would have been looked down upon and excluded. To be content, you had to fulfill your role and forget living out your individual choices and desires. Today, we have the freedom to shape the direction of our own lives and our happiness. However, this new-found freedom also poses a new challenge. We must take more responsibility for our well-being and destiny. If you are unhappy, does that mean that you are responsible?

This next point applies to everyone but especially millennials or those part of the younger generation. You will have been raised in the social media world of constant self-judgement and online praise, receiving dopamine spikes every time somebody likes your content. Dopamine is a feel-good hormone, released to reward us. Social media can be causing serious harm to your health and happiness. Detaching from these addictive technologies will reverse some of the damage caused to you or your children and will benefit your day-to-day happiness in a big way.

The genetic, environmental, cultural and generational differences are important to be aware of as not everything you do is through freedom of choice, even if it might seem so! With that in mind, it will be easier to develop happiness in your life and also allow you to understand the reasons behind differing approaches to happiness.

Happiness is Damn Important!

"We seek happiness in almost everything we do. Happiness is

undoubtedly the most important aspect of life."

Felix New

Maybe you can relate to some of the following scenarios:

Q: *Why do you go to the gym after work when you're already too tired to stand up straight?*

A: Because I want to be in shape. Being fit makes other people view me in a more attractive light and it gives me more energy. That makes me happy.

Q: *Why are you in this relationship? The single life is much more liberating!*

A: I love my partner. Being with them makes me the happiest person alive. They are my everything. They make me happy and I want to see them happy.

Q: *Why do you practise gratitude and meditation? You tryna be a monk bro?*

A: I want to calm my mind and be content in life. A calm state of mind is fundamental to happiness for me. I want to be happy in this life to serve the world better.

You will always find happiness somewhere within your answers. I challenge you to find more than five questions about what people do where the root answer doesn't have something to do with happiness. Sometimes it's buried deep, but it's in there somewhere. Happiness is the underlying motivation for almost anything and everything we do!

Over 2,000 years ago, Aristotle said seeking happiness was the primary purpose of life. I don't want to call myself a modern-day Aristotle, but I do agree with the guy. The world's most prominent religions and philosophies focus on achieving a state of happiness and contentment. In 2012, The United Nations even declared the 20th of March as *Happiness Day* to recognise happiness as a universal goal. The Dalai Lama also tells us that to be happy is the main purpose of life.

Where are all my American readers at? If we take a look at the American Declaration of Independence *Life, Liberty and the Pursuit of Happiness* are described as unchallengeable rights. There seems to be a notion among people in western societies that happiness needs to be *earned*. That is complete nonsense. The fact we have consciousness flowing through us is enough of a reason to allow ourselves to be happy. Anything else you achieve is a nice addition to your life, but certainly not a certificate for happiness.

In the realm of happiness literature, people often say *Happiness is your birthright*. This doesn't mean you shouldn't strive to be the best you can be, it just means you should always be kind to yourself and enjoy the process of getting to wherever you want to be in life.

Happiness Isn't All That Matters

Individual happiness is damn important, but it's not all that matters. It's also important to live a good life by spreading good in the world.

If we all seek happiness in an egotistical fashion, the world wouldn't be such a pretty place. For myself, I aim to positively influence as many people as possible with my writing, music and actions - not being the cause of people's suffering. I'm here to serve the world while still acting dignified and looking after my own happiness.

What is important for you besides individual happiness? Maybe write it down or make a mental note of it.

_____

_____

_____

What Science Says and Why You Should Care

Having many doctors in my friend group, I have always been careful in the scientific claims I repeat. In my body-building days, I would have countless discussions on the scientific proof of why eggs are good or bad for you or why gluten can give you belly fat. Despite it being slightly frustrating at times to debate with people who have centuries of medical knowledge under their belt, this has made me more conscious of the scientific evidence I use to back up the claims I make.

Does science say happiness is important?

For thousands of years we have been trying to find ways to live longer. According to new studies, happiness could be the key to longevity. Not only does an increase in happiness make people feel good mentally but according to a recently published study in the scientific journal *Age and Ageing,* it is said to substantially reduce all-cause mortality among older people. Happier people are said to be in better physical health and experience lower mortality rates. Happiness lowers the levels of cortisol (the stress hormone), strengthening our heart and immune system and much more. I've even heard that happy people live up to 10 years longer and have 35% less chance of dying in the next five years. If it's true, the medical profession needs to take a close look at the benefits of being happy, especially in old age.

You guessed it, that sounded too good to be true! The link between happiness and living longer also has its critics. Published in *The Lancet,* a 10-year study of one million women claimed there is no link between unhappiness and mortality. In fact, the researchers say that previous studies mixed up cause and effect. Arguing instead that it was ill-health that made people unhappy and not vice versa. Future studies will need to investigate both sides of the coin, but personally, I'd rather not be a grumpy chap. Maybe I'll live longer in the process!

How Do I Focus?

This fantastic move towards seeking happiness has its downsides. Now that more of us are seeking happiness, there's been an explosion of the happiness industry and many conflicting opinions. An increase in coaching, books and seminars make it increasingly hard to navigate through this terrain. What's the best way to meditate? Should I use affirmations? Do I need to go on retreats? Do I need a spiritual teacher or mentor?

Don't get too overwhelmed. Stick with only a few books and mentors who resonate with you. Don't buy every single book on happiness. If the few resources you select are high quality, you will soon feel your life change in unimaginable ways. You can slowly add more material if you need it. I know so many people who were left speechless by realising the power they have to change their lives for the better. For me, the combination of Eckhart Tolle and Prince Ea did a lot to guide me on my happiness journey. I never went on any expensive retreats. I just acquired knowledge and good mentors. The underlying principles to happiness are fairly straightforward. Although, finding a good therapist to work through traumas can sometimes be an essential part of healing and somewhat of an exception here.

A few weeks ago, a friend brought me back a small souvenir from her holiday. It's a colourful badge reading the words *WHATEVER YOU DECIDE TO DO, MAKE SURE IT MAKES YOU HAPPY*. The quest for happiness is everywhere, even in Italian souvenir shops!

The Problem with Happiness

Is it a problem that we are all after the same thing? Not at all. There is enough happiness for each of us; it's an infinite resource! Happiness can't be used up.

What does your happiness have in common with a rich oil company from the Middle East?

I'm sure you've heard about how rich oil nations extract seemingly infinite oil and convert it into incredible riches. With happiness, it's no different. You have an abundance of happiness within you. Unlike oil, it's an infinite resource and much better for the planet. We're not necessarily the winners in this example because the rich oil companies are much better at extracting from their source. They know how to effectively get to that oil and convert it into currency. The problem is, many of us are not finding happiness. Many of us get frustrated on our search and as a result, pull others down too. We do this by making mean remarks or even getting physically violent to let out our frustration. The problem with happiness is the belief that, *if I can't have it, then you shouldn't have it either.*

We have not been taught about the tools we need to extract happiness or even the simple advice on where to extract it from. Many of us are looking for it in the wrong places. Instead of finding ways to extract the happiness from the abundant source within, people are looking to extract it from unattainable sources outside of themselves. These materialistic desires are comparable to the boss of a rich oil company going to a small puddle to source all the oil his company needs. The chances of finding oil or finding *enough* oil are very close to zero. An unattainable mission.

According to the World Health Organization, more than 300 million people are affected by depression, making it the leading cause of disability globally.

A 2018 study by BlueCross & BlueShield showed how the diagnosis of major depression had risen 33% since 2013 amongst Americans, especially among younger people.

Why do we think we'll find happiness if we follow a path that has not been working so far? Why do we keep trying to extract happiness from this external source? Digging deeper still won't get us there. There is nothing to extract. Why do we keep going back to the same old puddle?

As a result, many of us don't feel happy for a good portion of time. Let's be real - we should be ECSTATIC. We now have devices where we can access all of the information we've ever needed within seconds. Medical advances allow us to live longer than ever before. We can travel anywhere in the world within 24 hours without it costing us an arm and a leg (literally). Yet, this doesn't seem to bring us enough happiness. In fact, many of us are often straight up miserable, always worried about yesterday, today and tomorrow.

There's another group within our ranks, and maybe you're one of them (if so, welcome). We might feel comfortable living in a nice house, having a decent job, and grinding away at the routines of life but many of us feel miserable yet too comfortable to change anything for the better. Comfortable, but certainly not happy most of the time. A sense of emptiness and longing for more always remains.

Are People Really Seeking Unattainable Happiness?

Next time you walk through a city at night, imagine you're an alien and it's the first time you're observing human behaviour. You'll see extreme manifestations of people looking to fill the void of unhappiness. You'll encounter drunks forgetting all their worries in a bottle. You'll encounter people dressed in flashy clothing to feel good about themselves. You'll need to be careful not to get run over by drivers racing down the high street hoping to get admiration for their metal box on four wheels. You see people spending more than they can afford on fancy restaurants and wine.

These ways of unwinding have become so normal for us that it's valuable to take an outsider's perspective from time to time. That doesn't mean we shouldn't indulge in these pleasures, but we need to be crystal clear about our motivation behind what we do. When you have developed your Happiness Button, you can certainly still dance to loud music, dress well and eat expensive meals − it will just come from a place of wholeness, not lack.

The majority view is that being on a journey of seeking happiness is something that alternative people, hippies or monks do. At the same time, everyone is on the path of seeking happiness by buying all these products and exclusive holidays. It's just masked behind consumerism and what is considered *normal*. What is cool about taking the unattainable path?

You certainly won't find any TV presenter cheering someone on for achieving an amazing state of gratitude or having had a very happy and peaceful meditation session (apart from Oprah maybe, she's into that stuff). Instead, you will see someone being cheered on for winning the lottery or downing the most beer in world record time.

If you look at the way many societies are structured, you'll realise that a lot of it is set up to make you unhappy. To keep the economy going and fill the pockets of big companies, there are countless messages instilled in your mind to make you worry and seriously unhappy. This is because people who are grateful for what they have, don't <u>need</u> to buy that much to keep them happy. It's assumed that happy people don't bring in as much money for big companies. Desperate and miserable people are the target instead. Offering happy people fulfillment through goods or services is like offering a monkey who lives in a banana tree, a banana!

Calm Down Felix; Maybe You're Just Overstating the Issue

A 2018 well-being report from The UK Office for National Statistics claims that people in the UK reported 7.5 out of 10 for happiness levels. They argue that happiness levels are increasing. Are people becoming happier? Is there any need for all of this?

Let's look at the flip side of the coin.

1. Life is getting more stressful, especially in the workplace. High

rates of income inequality, non-stop stimuli, student debts, decreased wages, decreased job security (30% of jobs at risk by 2030 due to automation) and an increase in the pressure to do well in life. Everything is expected to happen faster.

2. According to the World Health Organization, more than 300 million people are affected by depression, making it the leading cause of disability globally. A 2018 study by *BlueCross & BlueShield* showed how the diagnosis of major depression had risen 33% since 2013 amongst Americans, especially among younger people. While depression can run in the family, there will also be many people who drifted from unhappiness into depression.

3. The growth of pharmaceutical companies. There are millions of people who take 'happy pills' - trying to tackle unhappiness. Equally, employers and individuals have started to invest heavily in mindfulness programs such as courses and apps. The mindfulness industry is now a billion-dollar industry with steady growth. As much as I congratulate the move towards more mindful living, the popularity and the fact that employers are incorporating such programs shows the severe need to help people deal with unhappiness.

4. Look around you. Look how miserable a lot of us are. Speak to people and hear them complaining or sulking about something in their life. Pay close attention to it for a day. Imagine you're the alien again and this time you're just observing the daily commute on a regular workday. Look how serious and tense most people's facial expressions are. Look how deep their frowning wrinkles are running. Maybe even observe your own behaviour and expressions, is it influenced by the world?

Choices!

Nowadays we have too many choices and it's making us unhappy. In the past, choices were much more restricted. People knew what they could achieve and expect in their life and what was highly unlikely. Today, with people experiencing higher levels of affluence, more freedom to choose partners and achieve a dream lifestyle, things are in our own hands. Not only do we blame ourselves when something goes wrong, but we are also overwhelmed by all the choices that are presented to us. Researchers from Columbia and Stanford University found that when there were 24 different jams at a market stall, people were far less likely to buy jam than if there were only six options. Having too many options is counterproductive!

True Happiness is FREE but No Quick Fix

Although you can access happiness in this moment with gratitude or compassion, developing a long-term happy state of mind and relieving yourself from past emotional pains takes time and effort.

You must develop the right techniques and have certain realisations about your life. You need to learn to recognise happiness and not silence or ignore it. It isn't as easy as just buying something. Building up your happiness from within doesn't take *that* long. You'll continue to feel happier along the way and it's 100000% worth it! You can look at it as an investment for the rest of your life. Plus, it's *sustainable* unlike the dopamine gained from purchasing material goods.

You might be thinking that this is for people who have lost touch with the world, live in the forest, say *ohmmm* and drink herbal tea all day. I used to think the same thing whenever people would say "happiness is within you". *Well, where is it then??? Next to my liver or maybe my left kidney?*

No one I admired or looked up to when growing up ever mentioned that happiness is always available to us. Instead, they would talk about reaching for your dreams until you have a lot of wealth or a perfect relationship. Internal happiness was a strange illusionary concept to me. Funny how time flies. I recently recorded a song with an amazing artist called Luke Truth, where he sings, "look inside and you'll find all of the treasure."

Money Matters

Money matters for happiness! Yep, I said it again!

We already talked about how environmental factors can shape our happiness, but since the questions around money never stop, I just wanted to say a few last words on it so we can settle this debate once and for all.

My understanding is that you can be happy with very little to your name. However, for many of us having very few resources will make being happy much harder. On your happiness endeavour, try to get smart financially to free yourself from struggle, and build up enough so you can give back to people who need it most. Great books to help with this are *Money: Know More, Make More, Give More* by Rob Moore or the classic *Rich Dad Poor Dad* by Robert Kiyosaki. Although money can take some weight off your shoulders, you'll find that what fulfills you is never the money itself but the fact that you are providing value to the world and have a reason to get up in the morning. The money is a by-product if you're living a purposeful life and providing value to people.

I can feel how excited you are to start building your Happiness Button, and that's great! However, there are two crucial points we need to cover before we can start building.

The Unconscious Mind

Two years ago, I was sitting in a café enjoying a sweet potato soup with a cup of green tea (the Felix New diet). Unexpectedly, I felt the urge to strike up a conversation with the stranger sitting next to me. We connected exceptionally well from the get-go. We talked about our favourite foods, the power of the sweet potato and shared some absurd facts about life. For instance, the fact that Gary Kremen, founder of the popular online dating site match.com lost his girlfriend to a guy she met on match.com.

Then something strange happened. I don't know how or why but I started making a few critical remarks that brought the conversation to an abrupt end. You can ask anyone that knows me, and they will attest that I'm not a rude person. Far from it. Equally, I had no dislike for this woman at all. So, what had happened?! Why did those negative remarks arise? Why did I do it?

While reflecting on the situation at home later that

day, I realised what could have been the root cause. Deep down, I must have thought to myself; *this is too good to be true, no one can be this nice. They are just a stranger and strangers have sometimes acted rude to me. Maybe this woman has some negative intentions, masking them with her kindness and knowledge about sweet potatoes.* A fear of the unknown and lack of trust for a stranger propelled me to act unkindly. Although these were not thoughts that crossed my conscious mind, the interaction with the stranger triggered an unconscious reaction. A previous event must have instilled in me a mistrust of strangers.

Has this ever happened to you? Have you ever acted completely unreasonable and you weren't sure why?

Unexplained destructive behaviour is also *very* common in relationships as strong feelings can amplify unconscious insecurities. Imagine two people who are in a perfect relationship, Tom and Jenny (or Jerry if you like). They have a wonderful relationship, but Tom often overthinks everything Jenny says or does. He doesn't do it on purpose, it just happens. One night, he completely breaks down as Jenny comes home from work because she doesn't greet him or hug him before she goes upstairs to get changed. She was extremely exhausted and didn't want Tom to see her like that. *Does she not like me anymore? Is she cheating on me?* For the rest of the week, Tom is upset and lets Jenny feel it by ignoring her texts and coming home later than usual. After two months, a perfect relationship became filled with hate, fear, and resentment until the two split up. All their friends were shocked, as they seemed like the perfect match (no, they didn't meet on match.com).

Why the hell do we do that?

To understand why we unwillingly sabotage our

lives, you need to be aware that at a basic level there are two parts to how our mind functions. The conscious and the unconscious mind. Your conscious mind is the thinking part of the mind that's clearly visible to you. The unconscious, or subconscious mind, is not available to your awareness. It can still be the source of thoughts and emotions, but you are unaware that they stem from your unconscious so falsely believe them to be part of reality. No one can blame you, why would you not believe something that presents itself to you as reality? Mixed with a bodily reaction such as your chest or fist tightening up, it will seem even more real. You might not be aware of it, but your unconscious mind is a giant database filled with negative memories, traumas and pain that regularly resurface when they are triggered by events in your day-to-day life. In the example of Tom and Jenny, the relationship starts to crumble as Tom overthinks and projects negative thoughts onto Jenny. Most likely, Tom unconsciously has a fear of abandonment which played out even in this great relationship. The unconscious mind can easily be triggered by a song, smell or even the absence of a hug.

A considerable part of these painful memories is built up in childhood when we are developing. Imagine I was wearing my baby giraffe t-shirt on my birthday and everyone suddenly told me how ugly it looked. It would leave a scar in my unconscious database. I might always remain a little self-conscious about my looks or t-shirt choice. These painful memories might include rejection by loved ones and friends or even bullying at school. Maybe Tom never received hugs at home and didn't feel loved when he was a child. When Jenny did something that could be perceived as *I don't love you*, Tom relives the pain of similar situations he experienced in the past.

All of us have some traumatic experience stored in our giant unconscious database that cover a broad spectrum of past experiences. This part of our mind does not only activate when something terrible happens to us, but it's also addicted to making us suffer and self-sabotage our lives even in joyful situations. Often the unconscious fear of the unknown tries to ensure we stay exactly where we are. We are surviving just fine right now, why risk it with a new seemingly perfect relationship that could turn sour?

Being aware of this is crucial for establishing a happier life. This understanding helped me make sense of so many of my past experiences. It helped me make sense of arguments I had with friends and partners and times where I would become upset and self-sabotage when everything was going well. I even understood why I was so critical of the sweet potato soup stranger.

What is the solution to tackling the pain and negativity stored in our giant database of the unconscious?

If our minds were like USB drives, we could simply delete all the negative information from our minds. Our mind can't simply wipe it out, so we need to think of something else. Further on, I will show you exactly how to challenge your unconscious self-sabotaging mind effectively.

The EGO

Whenever I climb, I am followed by a dog called Ego

Friedrich Nietzsche

Have you ever told people you don't have a pet? Well, then you've lied!

We all have a dog called *Ego* that follows us around all day. Oh boy, is he a hassle to look after and keep healthy. If you understand what the ego is and the role it plays in your mind, then you're already incredibly close to true and sustained happiness.

Often, when I ask someone what they think the ego is, this is the answer I receive (I may or may not be quoting a drunken guy at a bus stop I asked this question to at around 3am in the morning)

> *"Well, it's thinking you are the best – when someone has a big ego bro, that means they are very self-obsessed and think they are the best and most important person in the room bro...you know bro."*

Sure, our drunken friend raises some helpful points that flow into the ego, but the ego is so much more than that.

To understand the ego, you need to become aware of one life-changing fact.

You are not your thoughts (Nietzsche might have said 'You are not your dog').

If you're familiar with meditation, this will be nothing new to you but if you are not, then this one sentence could well change the rest of your life.

It surely changed mine. Are you ready to be shaken out of your bed, chair or wherever you are lounging?

In some way, your life is one big illusion.

Your conception of *I* or *Me* is what you think you are but how real is this understanding? Your ego is a creation of your intellect that started to develop in childhood when you first realised you're an individual who can go and eat as many cookies as he/she pleases. All thoughts about who you think you are constitute the ego including your name, ethnicity, likes, dislikes or any beliefs you may hold. How real is this conception of you? The majority of the western world fully accepts this mental construct to be a correct representation of who they are. However, we need to realise that our ego or understanding of *I* is nothing but a collection of thoughts that create a unique sense of self. As much as we all hate to admit it, who we think we are is a mental illusion.

It's about questioning how real this conception of yourself is. Can you start to let loose a little, and why should you aim to? Not all thoughts are created equal and while some are random and concern crazy badgers, some of our thoughts are highly destructive. One type of thought that often causes problems for us are those of fear. Ego-based thoughts often fear the unknown, uncomfortable or unsafe. This is because anything that could endanger the mental construct of who you think you are is a threat. For the longest time, I would get upset if people thought my ideas or music weren't good. My ego feared that the mental image of being a guy with good ideas or a decent musician could collapse and I would fall into uncertainty. So, my ego would put up a fight.

At an evolutionary level, your ego features the primitive mind. Our drunk friend from the bus stop was right about that. The focus of this survival mechanism is on fighting competitors to ensure you come out on top. If you fail to do well at something, the ego gives you a hard time. It tells you you're worthless. From an evolutionary point of view, this self-critiquing can be very helpful. It forces you to keep evolving.

When you're doing well, your ego rewards you by telling you; you're the best human to ever walk the planet. This is why famous and successful people are often said to have a big ego. The ego also shows itself as the 'inner critic' we all know too well. At times, the inner critic makes us suffer heavily as it can be pretty mean. It tries to save you from embarrassment, hurt and abandonment as these could risk your survival. It self-sabotages to avoid the unknown. Taking a step back from the ego can minimise unhappiness. The goal shouldn't be to destroy the ego. We just need to ensure that it doesn't make us suffer. Learn to work *with* the ego, not *against* it.

In this book, you will learn to recognise when your ego kicks in. Once you have become aware of the ego, you will be able to distinguish it from the real you. Don't worry if it's too much to take in right now. You will learn how to master this skill of 'disarming the ego' effectively. You cannot achieve sustained happiness if you fully identify with the ego. You simply can't.

CLOSING THIS CHAPTER
(but feel free to come back to it)

If you are to develop true happiness, you need to have a good sense of what happiness means and how it's explored. I aim to leave you with a clear blue-sky understanding of happiness. *It is never too late to be happy* as Jane Fonda says. Just by reading this chapter, you'll already have some tools to protect yourself when the world or your mind tries to make you unhappy. Now, let's build up your happiness arsenal with the seven steps to happiness. Let's build your very own Happiness Button.

ADDITIONAL RESOURCES

Want to know more about the tricky concept of the *ego*? Fascinating books on this topic are *Conquer your inner voice* by Robert and Lisa Firestone *or Taming Your Gremlin* by Rick Carson.

CHAPTER 2: HOW TO DEVELOP YOUR HAPPINESS BUTTON

Now, the moment you've been waiting for. This is the blueprint for your Happiness Button!

Break-down of Happiness Button

> "We are what we repeatedly do. Excellence, then, is not an act, but a habit."
>
> **Will Durant**

This is your Happiness Button. You can see each one of the essential steps symbolised by an avatar. This should help to visualise each step.

Presence (The Meditating Monk) – Chapter 3

Acceptance (The Drooping Flower) – Chapter 4

Gratitude (The Thankful Hands) – Chapter 5

Affirmations (The Arm Flexing Its Guns) – Chapter 6

Compassion (The Listening Ear) – Chapter 7

**Enjoy the Journey & Embrace
Change** (The Footprints)   –
Chapter 8

**Face your Fears & Negative
Emotions** (The Not So Scary Ghost)   –
Chapter 9

On the outskirts, fuelling the Happiness Button, you have the launching rocket, the **Additional Steps** to happiness to be found in Chapter 10 (also known as happiness boosters!).

You might have noticed that some of the elements are bigger than others. For example, the meditating monk is bigger than the ghost. This symbolises that this person is currently spending more time being present than facing their fears and emotions. This will shift all the time as you figure out what works best for you or what area needs more attention.

Your Happiness Button is Unique

We are all unique and amazing human beings. Although we have many similarities, we also function differently too. There is not ONE Happiness Button, and there is not only one way to develop it. For some, gratitude will be the most effective way to increase happiness while for others compassion might be the most effective. That's all good, just be open to what comes!

You have the freedom to personalise the steps for yourself. You can adapt your approach accordingly and find a beautiful and effective path to happiness that works for you. Familiarise yourself with what each step entails and complete your daily practices. Remember, you can always refer back to the book when you need a refresher.

How to Apply the Steps?

At the end of the book, we have the #MyHappinessButtonChallenge which is a 30-day challenge (optional) that helps you take immediate action in applying the steps to happiness you will discover. If you prefer to move at your own pace, you can do that too. Whatever works for you.

How Will You Know Your Happiness Button is Taking Shape?

You will start to feel happier! You will feel that things don't irritate you as much as they used to, you will smile more, and you will find yourself in fun little conversations with strangers. It's magical. You will feel happiness streaming throughout your body. You will be full of joy and appreciation for this amazing life. You will begin to feel a true sense of happiness that carries through your day. Make the most of this book (and life).

It's time for us to roll up our sleeves and get to work. By just reading through the pages of the next seven chapters, you will surely take in some useful and insightful information.

If you want to feel genuine and sustainable happiness, you'll need to take action to apply what you discover. If you don't approach life with openness, you won't experience many changes. It's okay to move forward at your own speed, but you need to move forward.

Life is too short to be a passive observer.

Why Am I Being So Dramatic About Taking Action?

I've seen it time and time again in my own life and the lives of others. We get excited about a book, lecture or workshop, remember what we learned for a few weeks, try out one or two new things and then quickly fall back into our old ways of life. I heard a statistic that says 90% of people never fulfil the lessons they've learned through 'self-development' content. That's crazy! What did you spend the money for? Why did you take the time to attend the workshop and turn down your sister's birthday party invite?

Why Do We Ditch This Valuable Information?

Most people like the feeling of buying books or services that will supposedly help them solve a problem in their life. Of course, such first steps are commendable but when it comes to committing to something new outside of our comfort zone, we drop out and forget the lessons we've learned. Life can get busy and overwhelming. It's hard to integrate discoveries as part of our daily habits and routines. It seems as if it requires too much effort. Trying to fit in this new stuff next to the struggles of paying bills, managing annoying relatives and coping with the stress at work might feel the same as trying to nail jelly to a tree. It's just easier to continue living the way we've been living than to change our ways.

Staying Committed

Don't fear, my friend. Not all hope is lost. Let's ensure we are part of that 10% who take action to change their lives.

- **Form Habits!**

"We are what we repeatedly do. Excellence, then, is not an act, but a habit."
Will Durant

Forming new habits in your life is possible, and it's not that hard if you know how to do it. Repetition is key. If you wish to make running a habit, you'll need to be strict with yourself initially. Don't miss a day, and don't break your promise to yourself. Break a sweat but not a promise. Once the hardest first week or two is over, it will become easier and eventually more effortless. All you need to do is repeat the action often enough before it becomes part of your routine. A common myth assumes that it takes 21 days to form any habit. Although you might well develop a habit in three weeks, this is not guaranteed. We all function a little different. How much mental effort does it take to convince yourself to brush your teeth? Ideally, not very much. It can be the same for the steps to happiness such as meditation or practising gratitude.

Habits are what makes you *excellent.* Without positive habits, you will fall back into old ways of living, and your life will never change. It's up to you, excellence or mediocrity?

At the end of the book, we have the #MyHappinessButton-Challenge which is a 30-day challenge (optional) that helps you take immediate action in applying the steps to happiness you will discover. If you prefer to move at your own pace, you can do that too. Whatever works for you.

- **FOCUS!**

  "Aim higher. Stay focused."
  - **Brandon Adams**

Stop jumping from one thing to the next. You will never achieve change when you keep moving on to the next cure without giving one method a chance. When you take antibiotics to cure an infection, they don't work if you ditch them after taking them a few times. Catch yourself out when you are moving from cure to cure and remind yourself to finish carrying out one before moving on to another. Don't just nibble, enjoy the whole meal ☺.

- **Don't Be Part of the 90%!**

Remind yourself as often as possible that you don't want to be part of the 90% who waste the knowledge they gain. You want to make use of that hard-earned money and time you've invested. You want a return on your investment. You don't want to settle for being an average and passive person. Write a Post-it note and put it next to your bed or fridge: **Say-No-to-90%** or **Be-the-10%**

Let's stay committed. Let's congratulate ourselves and others for any achievements, however small they may be. Let's form habits. Let's build our own Happiness Button and lift each other up in the process. Let's create a community and start a movement to make this world a happier place!

CHAPTER 3: PRESENCE

It's a bright sunny day. You open the front door and step outside to enjoy the warmth and fresh breeze. You decide it's the perfect occasion to take a walk around the neighbourhood. On the broad street, you see children playing with water pistols and running for the ice cream truck. The more the truck rings its bell, the more children seem to be emerging from their houses. You never knew so many kids lived on your street!

You take a couple of deep breaths and start walking. You admire the awesome Ford Mustang that drives past you (maybe it's the guy from chapter 1). Without noticing, you become lost in thought, thinking about everything on your to-do list. It's not long until

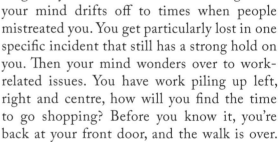

your mind drifts off to times when people mistreated you. You get particularly lost in one specific incident that still has a strong hold on you. Then your mind wonders over to work-related issues. You have work piling up left, right and centre, how will you find the time to go shopping? Before you know it, you're back at your front door, and the walk is over. Something sticky is on the sole of your shoe. In your absent-mindedness, you stepped in chewing gum. Your head is not much clearer than before. Apart from a bit of oxygen, old chewing gum and some exercise, you haven't taken much joy from your walk.

Does This Sound Like You?

Most of us spend our day caught up in thought. As a result, we miss out on much of our life as it's taking place. For far too much of our time, we <u>are **here**</u>, physically but <u>not **here,**</u> mentally.

Is There A Way Out?

"Whatever has happened to you in your past has no power over this present moment, because life is now."
Oprah Winfrey

When you learn how to be present, it's often an instant relief from unhappiness. Developing presence in your life is quite possibly the most fundamental and transformational step to happiness. Numerous people have told me that presence is the most powerful step they've discovered, and I certainly agree.

But Hold Up Felix, *What* Is Presence?

Presence is living fully in the moment. Living in that blissful sweet spot of life that moves beyond the mental hold of the past and the worries of the future. It's a state of peace and ease of being. Does that sound too good to be true? Well, it has to be true because you've experienced it before. When you were a child playing outside with your friends, watching a beautiful sunrise or eating delicious food, doing what you love, being in a state of 'flow'. In those moments you fully experienced everything without getting lost in your thoughts. The smell of flowers, the taste of pepper on your pizza, the feel of guitar strings, the breeze. You might not have been aware, but that was **presence** you experienced.

But Then We're Faced with Real Life...

Everyday life results in us being too busy or worried to tap into the present moment. No one ever educates us about the possibility of stepping out from this constant chatter of the mind. Wouldn't it be amazing to enjoy our life fully? When you tune into the present moment, it's possible!

Destructive Thoughts

Destructive thoughts take us away from the present moment with serious force. They eat away at our happiness every time we engage in them. If you were Superman, they would be your kryptonite as it takes away a lot of your power to be happy. Self-destructive thoughts don't just pop into our head randomly throughout the day, they are very often created directly from a situation you experience.

For example, you plan to have a friendly conversation with a person you wish to know better. When you see them, you freeze up, nod and swiftly walk past. Your negative self-talk kicks in immediately, blaming you for being too shy and telling you how much of a failure you are. *If you can't even talk to this person, how will you ever make new friends?* Practising how to be more in the present moment strongly reduces the frequency of destructive thoughts popping up, regardless of the situation you're in. Negativity is replaced with kinder and calmer thoughts.

How Presence Changed My Life

When I was recovering from glandular fever and post-viral fatigue, I really didn't have much going on in my life. I couldn't do much work, I didn't have a social life and I had no idea if I was ever going to get better. In hindsight, I had plenty to be grateful for but my almost depressed self, didn't see that at all. There was something I did have, however. The present moment a.k.a Mr. Life-Saver. My purpose was just to 'be here right now', truly experiencing and being calm in every moment without letting my thoughts drive me crazy. I told myself: *Let me be present to this moment. See what comes up. Forget the past or what will happen in the future. Everything else will come with time.* Now I have a career doing what I love, great friends to spend time with and perhaps most importantly, good health. All of this seemed like a light in the far distance back then, but presence carried me through the difficult times.

A Happiness Button Exercise

The present moment is free from worries and anxieties.
The present moment is full of gratitude and happiness.

Write down this reminder on a post-it note.
Put it somewhere you can see it every day.

Thanks to presence, it takes a lot to shake my mood these days. Ever since I've strengthened the ability to bring my awareness to the present moment, I have massively reduced worries about the future, negative feelings about the past and general negative self-talk. Now I thoroughly enjoy the simple things in life. Sometimes it almost feels ecstatic to be alive, even when I'm doing something others might see as mundane, such as walking down a regular street. When someone tries to intentionally or non-intentionally irritate me, I try to bring my awareness back to the present moment without getting caught up in a spiral of anger and negative thoughts. It might take some getting used to, but being present feels like being 'high on life'.

The Moment I Rediscovered Presence...

Although I had experienced many bursts of presence in my life, I never associated them with 'presence', not until I picked up *Mindfulness: A Practical Guide To Finding Peace In A Frantic World* by Danny Penman & Mark Williams. The book included a CD with guided meditations. Being naturally curious, I popped in the CD and started to meditate for the first time. Did I suddenly lose all my hair, find myself wearing an orange robe and become a monk? Certainly not, although that would have been a pleasant surprise for my family and friends.

I did, however, experience presence at a whole new level. I was amazed that there was a world out there and a way of living life so peacefully and happy that I had learned nothing about in school. Yes, running across endless open fields as a child (like the UK's current PM) was very blissful but I didn't know that adults could experience such feelings too. I saw the potential of a path to free myself from my worries and anxieties. Then life got in the way and I forgot about what I discovered. In law school, we might hear about mediation, but meditation certainly wasn't a frequent topic.

It was the moment I picked up *The Power of Now* by Eckhart Tolle that everything started to change. Reading this book made me ask important questions and find many answers. It taught me about the ego, and the beauty of being present.

Eckhart Tolle goes on to describe presence as the primary purpose of life. I find something very calming and satisfying in looking at life in this way. Whenever you are present, you are fulfilling a large part of your purpose on this earth. Can you feel some weight being lifted off your shoulders?

Committing to presence doesn't mean that your career or relationships are unimportant. Just like on an airplane, you are told to put on your own oxygen mask first. You need to take care of yourself before you can start thinking about helping others. Once you pay more attention to being present, everything else falls into place because you have clarity. That was certainly the case for me.

You shouldn't stress about being the best at being present. Once we strive to be the best, the ego and the thinking mind step in to run the show, and thus defeat your purpose of being present. *Just chill, be present as much as possible and everything will flow from there!*

Balance

When I first read *The Power of Now*, I let go of everything and wanted to be present 24/7. I didn't find that to be particularly healthy for my mental well-being (and wallet), as although being focused on presence was great, I felt that I was missing a wider purpose. It's about balance. All aspects of your life should be fused with your dedication to presence.

Mindfulness

You might have heard someone saying 'mindfulness' in your friend circle, workplace or perhaps in a YouTube advert telling you to breathe reeeeeal slow. You might also have felt intrigued but not concerned enough to ask Mr. Google what it means and how it has helped people live happier, more fulfilling lives.

Mindfulness draws on ways of living that have been used in the East for centuries to live happier lives. It is essentially the act of being aware of the present moment, while also accepting any thoughts, feelings or physical sensations that might come up. An American professor of medicine called Jon Kabat-Zinn brought it to the Western world by developing the 'Mindfulness-Based Stress Reduction' (MBSR) programme and Centre for Mindfulness in Medicine. Hard to imagine that only a few years ago this was all new stuff.

As so many of us have never been taught about presence growing up, this increasing drive towards Mindfulness is probably the most useful and helpful invention for our physical and mental well-being since chocolate fountains (joke). When you use the presence part of your Happiness Button, you will be practising Mindfulness. Yes, you'll become one of those people. But that's okay, what's not boss-like about taking back control over your well-being and life?

Felix, I Can't See Myself Becoming A Hippy...

Presence is not just for hippies, hipsters and monks. The best-selling author and multi-millionaire investor, Tim Ferris interviewed 100's of highly successful people from Arnold Schwarzenegger to Jamie Foxx for his podcast and found that over 80% of them practise mindfulness. Surveys suggest that globally, around 200-500 million people meditate, surely there must be a good reason for it. Not only will presence make you happier, but it will also contribute towards your success!

But Won't This Take Years and Years?

Although you won't be a master overnight, you can experience positive effects right now. I'm just an 'average guy' and it worked for me. It will take you a little practice to tune into the present moment, but you'll get better at it all the time. Just keep at it. Rome wasn't built in a day, was it?

Steps to Happiness via Presence

DEVELOP 'THE OUTSIDER'S VIEW'

Thoughts continue to arise in your mind as always but instead of taking these thoughts to be YOU, take the perspective of an outsider looking into your mind. As a result, you gain distance from your thoughts.

A thought comes and goes, and another comes and goes, without you identifying with them you then view the problems and worries that stem from your thoughts as distant creations of the mind and not reality!

Powerful stuff, eh?

Now, I hear you saying, "but I like the way I think, it makes me who I am. Can't I identify with my thoughts? Please, Felix, just make an exception for me." I hear you. Our minds are fantastic, and some thoughts we have are straight up genius or hilarious. Fully identifying with them wouldn't be as bad if it wasn't for negative thoughts. Often stemming from the unconscious database of past traumas, these thoughts take you far away from the present moment and into dark, unhappy places. We can't predict when they will come. Sometimes they pop up seemingly out of nowhere. Sometimes they are triggered by an event, sound or smell (think back to Tom and Jenny).

"Given that we have 10's of thousands of thoughts a day, we all have too many thoughts! The only difference for people with a calm mind is their reaction to the thoughts they have. They've learned to distance themselves from the thinking mind. They have understood that thoughts are merely creations of the mind that come and go."

That's why it's necessary to have an outsider's view. This allows you to recognise thoughts coming and going, knowing that you don't *have* to entertain them. You have the choice. You don't open the door to every person or animal that passes by your house, do you? Why should it be different for your thoughts?

There is another amazing benefit of taking an outsider's view. What do people do when they know an outsider is watching them? They behave better. The simple fact that you are observing your thoughts already calms down your mind. You'll see what I mean when you try it for yourself.

An influential endorser of presence and the outsider's view is Noah Elkrief. Before he became a happiness coach, he was working on the trading floor at Goldman Sachs and even got accepted into MENSA. Now, he's a bestselling author, has 190k subscribers on YouTube and 20,000 visitors a month on his blog, liveinthemoment.org. Noah argues that thoughts are what make us unhappy. If we experience any suffering or negative emotion, he argues that all we need to do is take a step back. He says: "*happiness is what remains when we are not thinking about anything, when we are not giving attention to our thoughts*". This would mean simply enjoying the act of dancing rather than worrying about what others might think of how lousy we're dancing.

Many spiritual teachers and authors call the outsider's view, 'the watcher'. Many of us are extremely far from being the watcher or outsider. This was re-affirmed to me recently, as I was speaking to a good friend of mine about how much sleep we get at night. My friend said, "It's so annoying, I go to bed at 11pm but I usually don't fall asleep until 1am. I always have too many thoughts! ☹"

Feeling empathetic for my sleep deprived panda-eye looking friend, here's what I replied.

(and no, I didn't ask them to buy sleeping pills, that's not the person I am!)

> *"Given that we have 10's of thousands of thoughts a day, we **all** have too many thoughts! The only difference for people with a calm mind is their reaction to the thoughts they have. They've learned to distance themselves from the thinking mind. They have understood that thoughts are merely creations of the mind that come and go. In other words, your thoughts are not YOU, and my thoughts are not ME. The problem arises when we follow thoughts without the possibility of stepping away from them. That's when you've lost touch with the present moment. This is especially problematic at night when we suddenly become aware of how hectic our thoughts are. You are not your thoughts, my dear friend."*

How Do I Develop the Outsider's View?

1. **Meditation**

   One of the best ways to develop the outsiders view is through meditation. Meditation is the practice of watching your breath and thoughts come and go without engaging in them. If you do happen to get lost in a thought then you just bring your awareness back to the here and now without giving yourself a hard time. This daily practice actively strengthens the outsider's view.

2. **Ask Yourself: 'What Would I Do If I Had an Outsider's View'?**

   Ask yourself what you would do if you were to take the position of the outsider. How would you respond to the current situation?

How quickly would you let go of the current thought? When you imagine it, your mind takes you there! A neat little trick, eh?

3. **Question the 'Threat'**

   Is there really a threat here?

   One of the main reasons our mind holds on to thoughts is for survival. In the early days of humans, it was vital to keep thinking about a threat such a large predator chasing us, so that we could stay alive. If we forgot about the threat halfway through running, we would be eaten. Makes sense, right? Today, our mind still perceives threat and has the same response. When your boss yells at you, your mind thinks your existence is threatened. As a result, you can't stop thinking about how your boss yelled at you.

   Here's where the outsider's view comes in: *Is this really a threat to my existence? Or did I create it in my mind? If there's no threat, I can let go and act calm.*

   By all means, if a large predator is chasing you, please keep running and keep thinking about it! That's a real threat right there. Otherwise, question the threat and if it isn't one, let that thought go its own way. If you're still running, good luck!

4. **Keep Applying the Outsider's View**

   Now it's just a matter of applying the outsider's view as often as possible. You don't need any fancy tricks, just use it every day and feel yourself getting better at it. You manage to take a step back much more comfortable every time, and you learn to stop the cycle of thoughts in their tracks.

MEDITATION

Studies have shown that meditation practice can change the brain structure, and functions in extremely beneficial ways. For example, the part of the brain that's in charge of positive emotions (the left side) increased for regular meditators, while the part that is in charge of negative emotions (the right side) decreased! This is an overly simplified explanation of more complex structures of the brain, but you get the point – meditation is damn good for you.

Meditation is a powerful and natural force fuelled by the power of presence.

- Improves your relationships *(we can all use that one)*

- Enhances creativity *(sure, gimme!)*

- Strengthens immune system *(this was crucial for me during my illness)*

- Improves your energy levels *(again, much needed in these stressful times!)*

- Improves your self-confidence *(seriously, who wouldn't want this?)*

- Makes you kinder to others *(what the world needs desperately)*

How Do I Get Started?

Guided and non-guided meditations, paying close attention to your movement such as deep breathing, swimming or running can all count as being in a meditative state.

Now, although you might be thinking this sounds easy, it really isn't! It takes determination and persistent daily practice to get the full benefits. When you start, your mind will be racing but you need to keep going until you start to feel your mind calm down. It's like playing an instrument. We can all make some noise with a piano or guitar, but it takes time to learn something that sounds nice and doesn't have your neighbours on the brink of madness.

Why Focus on the Breath?

The breath is the force of life. Without it we could not live (well, duh Felix, I knew that!). With each in-breath, we are giving our body new life and with each out-breath, we are letting go of what no longer serves us. Paying attention to this process impacts on your mind, making you feel revived and alive –in the here and now! Our breath is one of the only bodily function we can control. When someone is experiencing a panic attack, focusing on the breath is often the only thing people can do to calm their mind. It works wonders to break the cycle of anxiety. The breath is absolutely key to your Happiness Button. Never underestimate its power. Be grateful for it.

How Long Should I Meditate?

Start with 5 minutes every day and work your way up. I meditate around 15 minutes in the morning and ideally, another 15 minutes at night. You don't need to make a huge time commitment, so there should be no excuses.

How Long Until I Feel the Benefits?

You'll feel immediate benefits. You'll be more relaxed and happier after you meditate. You might experience the full effects after four weeks but depending on you as a person and the busyness of your mind, this can be slightly less or more. When you meditate, your brain 're-wires' and new pathways are formed. This drastically improves your mood and makes you feel more relaxed. When the effects start rolling in, you will start feeling happy during the day 'for no reason'. People will ask you why you're smiling so much lately. There is a reason, it's called meditation and the sense of presence you have discovered!

Non-Guided Meditation

There are many non-guided meditations you can try. Let me tell you about my experience of a non-guided mindful breathing meditation. A good friend of mine dragged me along to a residential house close to where we lived. In the living room, we formed a small circle with five people facing a Buddha statue. Two older British men, dressed in what I assumed was traditional Buddhist clothing, ran the small group meditation. I had been meditating for some time by myself, but these guys taught me a non-guided exercise that I love doing and that has transformed my meditation sessions.

A Happiness Button Exercise

Your Posture:

1. **BACK:** Sit upright with your back straight (you can do it lying down but it's all about being aware and awake in the moment, so sitting is better)

2. **FEET:** If sitting on a chair, have your feet firmly on the floor. If

you are crossing your legs, then your feet are fine as they are

3. **ARMS:** Resting on thighs and relaxed

4. **HANDS:** On top of each other in the form of a cup

5. **HEAD:** Facing forward. Nice and straight

6. **EYES:** Open or closed. Closed is often preferred

The Practise:

1. Breath in (through your nose)

2. Breath out (through your nose)

3. Count 1

4. Breath in (through your nose)

5. Breath out (through your nose)

6. Count 2

...and so on... until you reach 10 and start over again!

You should focus on what happens in your body when you breathe in. Focus on the flow of air you feel coming into your nostrils, and your belly expanding. When you breathe out, focus on the flow of air you feel going out of your nostrils, and your abdomen falling. Whenever your mind wanders, just bring it back to fully feeling the sensation of breathing. Thoughts will pop into your head, that's normal. Be aware of them but don't get lost following them. Just let them pass as freely as they arise! If you do get caught in a thought, don't sweat it! Congratulate yourself for noticing and go back to observing the breath. No hard feelings, whatever happens.

A HUGE mistake I've often made during meditation was judging how well I'm doing. "Nice, today I've only got lost in thoughts twice" or "Damn it, I can't concentrate at all today, why did I even try meditating?" You get much more out of your session if you remain without judgement. The whole point of meditation is to practice accepting awareness. This is what will benefit you in your day-to-day life when life tries to bring you down. You'll be one cool cucumber. "Oh, that's a thought. There it goes on its way".

The principles I describe above feature in many other non-guided meditations, but for some alternatives or more advanced non-guided meditations, bookshops and Google are your friends (or e-mail me for recommendations). A popular one is also breathing in through your nose for four seconds, holding the breath for seven seconds and then breathing out through your mouth for eight seconds. This helps to calm your mind and body instantly.

Once you've become a boss at the meditation exercise I learned from the Buddhists, you can try it without counting by just focusing on your breath.

Guided Meditations

Apps

The *Insight timer* app is a personal favourite of mine which includes a meditation timer and a lot of free guided meditations. The mediation I've listened to the most is called, 'Simply Being – Relaxation & Presence' by Mary Maddux. It only takes 5 minutes, so works as a speedy exercise in the morning or at night. Another favourite of mine on *Insight Timer* is 'Get Your Glow on Meditation' by Melissa Amrosini. It's a 10-minute long session that has some relaxing music in the background which helps to stop your mind from drifting away.

Subscription-based services

Headspace offers a subscription service and has become popular with a lot of people around the world. It has over 6 million active users who seem to believe that it's a pretty awesome app worth paying for! In terms of guided meditations, *Headspace* does guide you more than other free apps as it's focused on teaching you the <u>skill</u> of meditation. *Headspace* have described their app as 'your gym membership for the mind' which is a nice way of looking at it. Meditation is training. You train every day, and you feel yourself getting more focused as a result. *Headspace* can be useful for those who prefer more guidance along the way, no shame in that!

In-person and online meditation courses

Courses are usually focused on supporting you with a daily habit or to delve into a specific area of your life. These courses are often affordable, focused and effective as creating new habits can be a struggle (I've been there!). In person, courses tend to run for 1-8 weeks, and it can be helpful to practice what you've learned at home.

Although the online option might sound strange and not exactly enlightening, you can do these courses from the comfort of your home and usually get excellent e-mail support from teachers along the way. *Master Your Mind* is a five-week course created by Giovanni Dienstmann, teacher and owner of the popular mediation blog *Live and Dare*. The course cuts out all the fuzzy stuff and gets straight to the point. Giovanni also offers a monthly subscription to his *Limitless Life* bundle, giving you the chance to have one-on-one coaching with him. So, if you need a little more guidance from the comfort of your home, this is an option you could explore.

You Can Become A 'Good' Meditator for <u>Free</u>

Although apps and courses can be useful, you don't need them to become a 'good' meditator. You need to see what works for you. If using mobile apps is not your thing, there are tons of YouTube videos with free guided meditations or you can purchase inexpensive meditation CD's and play them on your ancient CD player.

Meditation Is A Game-Changer

I strongly advise you to meditate every day. Even if it's just for 5 minutes. It will make a huge difference for your happiness. When I go without meditating for too long, I can feel my mood dampening, and I'm less present. Meditation is an essential part of my life now.

Think of it this way, you can probably run a marathon without training. It's possible, it would only take you forever to reach the finish line, and you might feel like dying along the way! Make it easier for yourself and put in that training for your mind every day. Meditation might even become the highlight of your day.

But wait, there's something you should know!

I like to keep it real with my readers. Some people will tell you to meditate and send you off on your way thinking that it'll be all sunshine and rainbows. It's not always sunny when it comes to meditation. Anything that has the potential to change your life, needs to be handled with a degree of care. Many of you will know Jay Shetty, the inspirational filmmaker and former monk. He recently released a video titled *Why Meditation Made Me A Bad Person*. In his video, he describes how meditation made him more manipulative and arrogant. This could happen to you too!

Meditation can shine the light of awareness on your 'bad' tendencies, and that can be a little difficult to face. Jay realised, however, that it was not meditation that was turning him into a bad person, it was instead raising awareness of what was already inside of him. That is the beauty of meditation. It shows you what areas of your life need to be worked on to become a better, happier person. As Jay says in his video: *before taking you to where you want to be, it will first take you to where you may not want to see.*

Most people have a very positive meditation experience, and it's life changing. What are you waiting for? It's time to check the prices of meditation cushions online. I tend to meditate on a matt or chair but I'm keen to get my hands on a meditation cushion (that's an excellent idea for a birthday gift for my friends reading this).

SEEING YOUR THOUGHTS AS 'TOOLS'

We think about the past, the future, and endless possible scenarios NON-STOP. We use our thoughts even when we don't need to be using them. What do you get when you try to solve a problem when there isn't one? A PROBLEM!

While you're out for a run, there is no need to use the thinking mind. It does not aid you in any way to run faster or longer. It only distracts you from your run and enjoying the fresh air or nice scenery around you. All your brain needs to do is to keep those feet moving and to look where you're going! Just be present and run. Feel your feet on the ground and watch the trees you are running past. Your run is your time to rejuvenate and gain new energy

Always ask yourself: *Do I need to be using my 'problem-solving tool' for what I am doing right now?*

If yes, use it to solve the situation. If no, then relax and focus on the present moment. If you can't complete planning or solving a problem then and there, then tell yourself you will come back to it. Put your thinking tool back in the toolbox and take yourself back to the amazing feeling of being in the present moment.

USE A PHRASE TO ZAP YOU INTO 'PRESENT MODE'

Sometimes, a simple phrase can bring you right back to the present moment. Let's say you're stuck in traffic and worried about being late, how you promised your friend you'd be on time, and then your mind drifts off to all those other times you weren't on time. Instead of getting lost in your thoughts for the whole duration of the journey, try saying these three words to yourself.

THIS IS IT. Life is right here in this moment. This moment is it. You better enjoy it, or you'll waste a precious moment of your life you'll never get back. There is always something great about being alive right now. Look at that cute dog that just poked its head out of the window in the car next to you. You are stuck in traffic, but you are breathing. You are alive. You are here right now. *This is it*.

A Happiness Button Exercise

Try saying *This is it* and see if you can spot something amazing about the present moment you are in right now. Try breathing slowing through your nose while doing so.

FOCUS ON YOUR FEET

It might sound strange but if you focus on your feet and the feeling of them on the ground, it literally grounds you (pun intended). This practice is often referred to as 'mindful walking'. Walking is so simple, yet amazing. Every step should bring you healing, joy, and happiness. If you can't walk, then still be present to the movement you do and the contact you have with any surfaces. Be present to what it feels like sitting and lying down or running your hands over your mobility assistance. Life is a miracle and truly awesome. *This is it*.

Gosh, if my 17-year-old-self heard me say 'walking is amazing', he would think I was a serious weirdo.

ACCEPTANCE

Acceptance and presence go hand-in-hand. When you get better at acceptance it will be easier to be present. Think about this – a bully will pick on the person who will give him the best reaction and most attention. The one who does not let the bully pull him into his negative world is relatively uninteresting to the bully. The better you become at acceptance, the calmer your mind will become. Try always to accept what you cannot change and if you can change it, plan and take action without wasting your time getting lost in too many thoughts. Go in, complete the task and get back to presence. Make the most of any given situation and move forward positively.

STEP BACK FROM THE EGO

It's important to note that the problem is never the ego itself. The problem is how we respond to it and the fact that most of us believe that we ARE the ego. We fully identify with the ego and think that these thoughts are simply the reality we need to face. This is a free ticket to the land of suffering. An ego-based thought merely is another cloud of thought passing by in the sky of your mind. Don't let it catch you.

"I think, therefore I am."
René Descartes

Who here has heard of this statement by Descartes? I read a funny re-phrase of this quote once which said, "Thinking, but there is no I." No ego, no I, but an awareness that thinking is going on. That's the sweet spot of presence.

It's beautiful when you have disarmed the ego (not killed) because any time a negative thought pops into your head, you can say "hey, this is the ego again and not reality" and go back to living your day, happily and peacefully.

Let's look at a real-life example to show you how you can practice disidentifying with the ego. This example is inspired by a good friend of mine who recently told me that he swears at least three times a day at other drivers.

You are driving, and you have almost reached home then suddenly at a crossing, another car emerges travelling at immense speed and you almost crash into each other. The driver opens the window and swears at you, calling you a bad driver, and telling you to watch where you are going. In response, you put your window down and get ready to yell that all of this is his fault and that you did nothing wrong whatsoever. You also want to tell him that he's an ugly toad.

Then, you realise that your ego has consumed you. The desire to be right and not let anyone endanger the concept of YOU has once again overcome you. So, take a mental step back and approach the situation more mindfully. Say to yourself, "I know I have good driving skills and the other guy was clearly driving too fast in his own anger". Mistakes happen. There's no harm done. I wonder what went wrong for him today that resulted in him being so angry towards me. What triggered his unconscious negative database?"

Stepping back is not about letting the other driver disrespect you. It's about not letting negativity infect you. Their ego is most likely running the show. Feel compassion for the guy and don't let his anger get you down. Don't let your ego take over your thoughts. Soon you will realise that 'winning' is completely irrelevant.

SURRENDER

You need to surrender to the present moment. You'll see that with acceptance and a peaceful attitude, your thoughts will stop trying so hard to fight for your attention. The negative self-talk will diminish drastically. Negative thoughts are no longer the enemy. They are just creations of the mind. Just like the Furby Toys are a creation and not based on reality (I hope!). When you wave your white flag of peace, life will also send back peaceful vibes to you. That's the beauty of it. You reap what you sow.

TAKE IN YOUR SURROUNDINGS

Are you in a room or out in nature? Just look around and admire everything about the location you are in. Be fully present. Does something catch your eye? Why do you think it caught your eye? Is it beautiful? Is it weird? Do you even know what it is?

Think about how long it must have taken to build the room. Think about how long it must have taken for the trees or hills to form. This exercise is even more dramatic when looking at old, historic buildings or when looking at picturesque nature. However, you don't need to travel to the pyramids to experience this feeling of awe.

Be grateful you can be here right now. Look at everything you previously took for granted in a new light. If you have never drawn on your ability to be present so actively before, it might feel like you are truly alive for the first time.

You might be thinking, "Okay, my suspicions were true, this Felix New guy is one of those woo-woo, airy fairy people." I understand that this sounds a little utopic but let's be real. We all miss out on a massive opportunity for happiness due to being stressed or lost in our minds. These small miracles are around us all the time - we just have to notice them.

So, where's the catch?

Yep, this is tricky and it might take some time to achieve but as I said, your ability will grow over time, and you will get better and better at it! Nothing worth having in life is easy.

Maybe you won't find it so hard, see what comes up! Please remember it's not a race. Regardless of your age, you don't need to have your life and happiness all sorted out by tomorrow. It's a process.

You <u>won't</u> get uncontrollably angry

You <u>won't</u> get easily offended

You <u>won't</u> get sad all the time

You <u>won't</u> have to think every thought that comes to you

You <u>will</u> make very wise and smart decisions/responses

You <u>will</u> make it further in life

You <u>will</u> have control over what thoughts you decide to follow

You <u>will</u> be happier!

IN A NUTSHELL

- Presence is living fully in the moment.
- Presence moves beyond the worries of the past and anxieties of the future.
- Often, we are *'here' physically, but not 'here' mentally.*
- Due to the busyness of modern life, moments of presence are rare.
- Destructive self-talk and negative thoughts pull us away from the present moment with strong force.
- You can see being present as your primary life purpose. Whenever you are present, you are doing amazing in life.
- Negative thoughts are reduced when we continue to tune into the present moment.
- Presence is possibly the most life-changing step to true happiness.
- You are not your thoughts. You don't need to think all that comes up.
- The outsider's view is your quickest way to step out of your thoughts.

- Meditation & Mindfulness help you become more present.

- With presence, you experience and enjoy life more fully (e.g. truly tasting that pizza).

- With practise, your ability to be present strengthens.

- When you are present, you notice the beauty around you!

- Presence & Mindfulness feature in the lives of most successful people.

- Tuning into presence isn't easy, but life is no race. It's well worth it!

- Tuning into the present moment changed Felix New's life. Will it change yours too?

SUMMARY OF STEPS

1. Develop 'the Outsider's View
2. Meditation (5 minutes a day or more)
3. Seeing Your Thoughts As 'Tools'
4. Use A Phrase to Zap You Into 'Present Mode'
5. Focus on Your Feet
6. Acceptance
7. Step Back from The Ego
8. Surrender
9. Take in Your Surroundings. Be in awe.

"Presence is the biggest present."
Felix New

That's my YouTube intro. Although I just pointed you to my social media, don't get me started on mobile phones and social media. These take us away from the present moment in alarming ways and must be used with care. I still remember waiting in front of a lecture at university and 95% of students were looking down at their phone instead of talking to each other. Despite this having become the norm in everyday life, I felt extremely sad to see it. I sometimes find myself getting pulled into these platforms, almost like quicksand, totally forgetting about the present moment. I'm sure you've experienced the same, but we will pick up on that later. Mr. Zuckerberg can wait.

CHAPTER 4: ACCEPTANCE

"Happiness can exist only in acceptance."
George Orwell (Novelist)

With some caution, what we might draw from the quote above is that if you can accept a situation, you can be happy. As American Author Werner Erhard put it, *happiness is a function of acceptance.* If we can manage to make our response one of acceptance, we will be at peace. That sounds great in theory, right?

I can hear you mumble, "but Felix, that's impossible."

I hear you. Acceptance is hard. Often, it's precisely the opposite of what we want to do. There are situations when it's tough to be accepting. When someone has seriously mistreated you or committed a terrible act. However, I will give you some tools you can use in everyday life to make it easier to practise acceptance in a natural and comfortable way. You will discover that even in difficult circumstances, there's often room for acceptance. Increasing acceptance in your life will undoubtedly bring you more happiness.

Happiness is a function of Acceptance.

Werner Erhard

Almost every time we suffer or struggle, it's because we can't ***accept what is.*** We wish things had played out differently in the past or we look anxiously towards the future. The true root of our suffering is rarely a situation or matter itself but rather our continued resistance to it. We need to learn to 'let it be' as the Beatles would say. Of course, it's incredibly difficult at times. I'm not blind to that. I've struggled with acceptance throughout my life and it's given me a fair share of suffering. However, reducing the resistance to acceptance is vital for sustainable happiness and inner peace. I heard you mumble a soft "okay, let's do this", so I guess it's time to dive into the world of cultivating acceptance!

The Basics of Acceptance

Often, the reason we get trapped in unhappiness is because we tell ourselves that our response of non-acceptance is reasonable. Well, if we get out the magnifying glass to look closely at the matter, how reasonable is it really?

All that happens when we don't accept is that we feel unsettled until we can change the situation. Even if we can improve the situation, when we have an attitude of blaming external circumstances for our unhappiness, another thing will come along before we know it and the cycle will repeat itself over, and over again. There will always be situations that are not to your liking and that you'll be unable to change, I promise you that. Even if you live on the perfect tropical island, you could get into an argument with a passing fisherman about who has the right to fish in these fine waters. Responding to events in your life with acceptance is a game-changer! When it comes to cultivating happiness, the only option we have is to remove ourselves from this cycle of non-acceptance.

Practising Acceptance

In March 2017, I boarded a plane in London and travelled 5,936 miles until I arrived at my destination, Tokyo, Japan. It was my first trip out of Europe, and I was extremely excited to explore this new land. What's something you need to do in Japan when you visit in springtime? Visit a cherry blossom park, of course! Metaphorically, the cherry blossom represents the strength, beauty and fleeting nature of life. Unlike most other flowers, the blossoms appears first and then the leaves follow. Symbolising a sense of becoming 'something out of nothing'. Equally, the cherry blossom demonstrates the fleeting nature of life, as it's full bloom usually lasts only up to a week. It reminds the Japanese people and visitors to value their precious time on earth and to be present to the beauty that surrounds them. As someone who loves deep inspirational metaphors, I was quickly sold and had to make my way to a park as soon as possible.

The next morning, I was walking through a park and admiring the not quite fully-blossomed flowers, trying to spot one that had fully bloomed and also trying my hand at vlogging. Thousands of new impressions had presented themselves to me in my first 24 hours. I must have surely looked disoriented trying to find my way in a country and culture I had never embraced before. At the same time, walking through this park was calming. I was enjoying the feeling of peace infused with the bitter-sweet aroma of the cherry blossom trees. I turned a corner and a monk approached me by putting a black beaded bracelet around my wrist and wishing me peace. "*My friend, you shall have peace, I wish you peace*".

He belonged to the nearby temple, and gave me a notepad where other visitors had written down their wishes and the amount of money they wanted to donate to maintain the temple. I could see Pete from Australia had wished for health and about ten other people from all over the world had wished for a better life for themselves and their loved ones. I was happy to help the temple; besides I liked the bracelet he gave me (still one of my favourites today). Experiencing more peace also sounded like a good idea. My naivety started to wear off when he asked me for a 10.000¥ donation (around $90 or £70). Aren't monks supposed to live very minimalist lives?! Asking for so much money from a single tourist seemed rude. I had another peek at the list he was holding and saw that apparently the other visitors had all donated that much. I could tell that something was fishy about this guy. I refused to pay the full amount and said I would give him 2000¥ (around $18 or £14). After all, maybe he was a real monk and people *did* donate substantial sums to the temple.

So, I gave him the money, and we parted ways. *Did I just help the temple, or did I get scammed?* It was when I saw a similar looking man approach another group of tourists that it all started to reveal itself. This man was dressed much less convincingly. His robe was dirty, and he had a severely ripped piece of paper in his hands. No doubt about it, I had fallen into the 'tourist trap' (ouch).

How could that happen to me? Why was I so stupid to believe him? I could have bought a seriously delicious

> We can always choose our response, even if we can't change a situation.

lunch for that money or some souvenirs for my family.

After some negative self-talk and a crushed ego, I soon came to some realisations.

1. Although the situation sucked, this was probably the most hilarious and strange story I could tell people about my experience in Japan.

2. I had a bracelet which was really cool (I am wearing it right now in fact). I probably would've bought it in a shop anyway.

3. I didn't pay all the 10.000¥, just 2000¥ which isn't the end of the world. It could have been worse.

4. The guy probably needed the money more than I did.

5. It won't happen to me again because now I know the trick and I will be more careful. In that sense, it's a small price to pay.

6. How is beating myself up about it going to improve anything? I don't want this incident to ruin the rest of my trip!

My mood changed instantly. I accepted what happened and tried to see the positive that came out of the situation. I was right, the story was the source of much amusement for my friends and family and even gave me a great story to share with strangers I met during my time in Japan. Overall, I was able to turn this situation of being scammed into something positive because I accepted it. (P.S. I Googled it. Apparently the fake monks got arrested a month after I was there).

The same technique of acceptance works for most other situations too. We can always choose our response, even if we can't change a situation.

"What you resist, not only persists, but will grow in size."
Carl Jung (Founder of Analytical Psychology)

What you accept, you can change. Change can mean

reframing the problem in your mind as something that holds some positive value. If you can't accept the situation and cling on to all the negative aspects of it, it will be challenging to transform your feelings about it into calmness and positivity. Over time, all this non-acceptance can become a serious weight on your shoulder that will dampen your mood.

Don't Sweep It Under the Rug!

Sweeping things under the rug is never a good idea. Repressed and unresolved feelings will resurface until they are dealt with. You must be open to what comes up. Life is not all sunshine and rainbows. Be accepting towards all that is but don't just push it away. For this chapter, the focus is on learning the skill of acceptance. Emotions that surface along with this are equally valuable and will teach us much about ourselves (see chapter 9).

A Happiness Button Exercise

1. Bring something to mind that is troubling you.

2. Tell yourself *I accept.... (insert you troubling thought/situation here) ... as it is. Worrying about it won't change the situation, if anything it will make it more negative. I allow myself to be free from the negative hold it has on me. I accept it as it is and instead, I choose to be calm. All is okay.*

3. Now try to find one thing that is positive about the situation. Bring this to mind and feel a sense of acceptance and relief within you. You can do that at any time of the day and with any situation that is troubling you. Long term or short term.

Once you have practised this a few times, you can move on to a more challenging exercise. Instead of finding a positive element to a situation, this is about accepting a given situation as it is.

1. So, repeat *I accept.... (insert you troubling thought/situation here) ... as it is. I allow myself to be free from the negative hold it has on me. I accept it as it is.*

Acceptance Is NOT Curling Up into A Ball and Giving Up

"Acceptance doesn't mean resignation; it means understanding that something is what it is and that there's got to be a way through it."

Michael J. Fox

Acceptance doesn't mean taking everything that life throws at you like a passive slob. If anything, it's the opposite. You start to take ownership of how you feel and don't let others determine your response. There are also times when you can and need to act to resolve a situation that troubles you. In those cases, you should take mindful well-thought-out action! If you can't act in the moment, plan ahead, accept what has happened and resolve it when you can. All that acceptance does is make you smart enough **not** to fall into the trap of continuous negative thoughts, and allow you to react to the situation with a cool and clear head.

The great thing is that acting from a place of acceptance and presence allows you to resolve problematic situations like a boss. If you're feeling boss-like now and would like to change clothes into something more eye-catching, feel free to do so.

Acceptance Is Living Like A Boss While Accepting Life

People often ask me how I manage to maintain such a positive outlook on life. I've thought long and hard about it. As I was trying to distil the reasons, the word 'acceptance' popped into my head. I guess that acceptance was the skill I developed to stay positive when I went through years of illness. Acceptance is a VITAL life skill.

Acceptance doesn't mean blanking out everything around you. A good boss is well aware of all that is happening in his environment, yet he doesn't let it distract him. I'm not big on swearing but I am big on giving credit where credit is due. John C. Parkin's book. *F**k It: The Ultimate Spiritual Way* has taught me a lot about acceptance. It hammered home the point that you can accept anything in your life. He argues that by saying F**k it to thoughts and situations, we start to enter a state of acceptance. I prefer to stick to 'It's all okay', but 'F**k it' certainly works well for some (and me too sometimes, let's be honest.)

The Next Level of Acceptance: Accepting & Loving Yourself

Acceptance goes deeper than a specific situation you might be facing. Do you accept yourself for who you are? Do you accept all your quirks and imperfections? (Remind you of John Legend's song 'All of me'?).

Have you dared to say the 'L' word to yourself?

Truly accepting and loving yourself for who you are is next level acceptance. In Pokémon terms, this would be a Charizard or any other highly evolved Pokémon.

If you don't accept yourself for who you are or what you look like, then you are providing your mind with the easiest way to come up with self-destructive thoughts. I know this might sound like a huge task as it means facing insecurities but when you start to accept yourself for who you are, with all your edges and 'flaws', that's when you enter serious happy land. If you can't change it, don't waste your time worrying about it.

Let's consider something many of us have struggled with. Our weight! I've certainly been there. I was chubby growing up. Nicknames like 'hamster cheeks' are a distant memory, but they happened and used to cause me suffering. If you are in a situation where you want to lose some weight (or gain), then acceptance will certainly ease the process for you. We often feel that we need to earn our right to love ourselves, but we need to unconditionally accept and appreciate ourselves for the beautiful human beings we are. With or without some extra pounds. This will take away the mental suffering. Of course, you might be causing serious damage to your health with your current weight. In such cases, you acknowledge that you need to change but at the same time, you accept and appreciate yourself. From this calmer state, you start to take action! You hit the gym or follow a fitness/dietary regime. You act and resolve the problem while accepting yourself each step along the way. That's the underlying mindset formula for a fantastic life filled with incredible levels of personal growth.

People sometimes ask me, "well do you love yourself?" My answer is usually, never a definitive YES or NO. Not because I don't love myself or I don't want to be seen as driven by my ego but instead because I feel that another answer is more helpful! "I'm learning to love myself more and more each day, as I discover who I truly am and accept what I discover".

There's a lovely lady you will meet in chapter 6, Mrs. Louise Hay. She says that the only thing that heals problems is knowing how to love yourself! Truly loving yourself is a lifelong job. It's not easy. Especially with images of perfect bodies and incredible careers plastered all over social media. In a song I wrote called *Surface*, I sing, "*we got to see beyond the surface, there's no such thing as perfect*". Not to toot my own horn but I think there's so much truth to that. Perfection is a made-up concept and highly based on individual perception, not any set-in-stone standard. That means we can choose if we see 'a flaw' as a flaw or as perfection. Acceptance means loving yourself because of your 'flaws' and seeing how truly remarkable you are – and trust me, you are. We all are!

> *They say one man's trash is another man's treasure and I say; one man's 'trash' could also be the same man's treasure if he practised acceptance.*

The choice is yours. I'm not asking you to be able to do this tomorrow. It's a process. Start by looking in the mirror and telling yourself you love and accept yourself for who you are. I mean that literally. Look in the mirror every day and tell yourself how beautiful you are, and how much you love yourself. I'm particularly looking at the men reading this who might resist the idea. You gotta do it man, it will change your life!

Acceptance Will Become Your (Slightly Addictive) Super-Power

Accepting a situation as it is or re-framing a situation (like the thug monk) positively, has now almost become a reflex and somewhat addictive to me. I love searching for the positive in situations like a detective - *Felix Holmes - finding the blessings in disguise*. People around me are always amazed at how I don't let negative situations bring me down, but it's because I have the tools to avoid the negative spiral and be positive. I allow and accept all that comes up. I don't resist, because I know it will persist otherwise! I am now passing the tools on to you to. You can directly and effectively apply them in your life using the steps below. Acceptance will become your new super-power, no need for all those superfoods to feel incredible. Toss those Goji berries to the side.

Steps to Happiness via Acceptance

USE A PHRASE TO ZAP YOU INTO ACCEPTANCE MODE

Do you remember the phrase we used for presence? Say it out loud now. If you don't remember, start turning back those pages! You can try using any of the following phrases to achieve acceptance.

1. All is okay.

2. It is what it is.

3. At the time, it seemed like the best thing to do with the information at hand. I can't change the past. Let me not ruin the present moment. It's all okay.

4. We are all human, we all make mistakes. It's all okay.

5. I accept what I can't change and decide to live peacefully instead. I allow all that is.

6. What I resist, persists, so I accept instead.

7. F**k it.

8. A word/phrase of your choice.

MAKE 'ACCEPTANCE' A LIFE GOAL

Make it a goal to live a life of acceptance rather than blame. Remind yourself of this daily. It's the path I chose. By doing so, you acknowledge that a life based on acceptance is so much more rewarding than a life based on (self) blame, (self) doubt and (self) shame.

Acceptance = Happiness
Blame, Doubt and Shame = Unhappiness

USE THE OUTSIDER'S VIEW

It can be hard to be accepting when your mind is running wild and playing out all kinds of scenarios. If you spot an ego-driven self-destructive thought, use the outsider's view we discovered in chapter three to stop it in its tracks. You're not stopping the thought itself, you are just adapting your response to it. Bring your full attention back to the present moment, to whatever it was you were doing before the thought entered your mind and go back to being accepting and calm.

BE KIND TO YOURSELF. FORGIVE YOURSELF

Let's say you made a mistake. Which you'll do all the time because you're human (unless you're an alien that picked up this book, then I apologise Mr. Alien).

Imagine you are vegan (for ethical not health reasons) and you happen to accidentally eat something containing cows milk. You could be mad at yourself for the next two weeks or you could be kind, forgiving and instantly relieve the tension. Use a phrase from Step One for example.

"We are all human, we all make mistakes. It's all okay."

You are aware of the mistake. You'll learn from it. Forgive yourself. Genuinely forgive yourself. Just as you would say to a friend who messed up. "Don't be so hard on yourself man, you'll do better next time. You couldn't have known there was milk in that. You'll be even more careful next time". Always try to be your own best friend speaking kind words of forgiveness in your ear. Accept that we all make mistakes, it's what makes us human.

REMIND YOURSELF OF YOUR MORTALITY

It might sound grim but nothing in this life is permanent. We will all die one day. Well unless someone creates a genius invention to keep us alive forever (I'm looking at you Mr. Alien). Just reminding yourself of the impermanence of life, you come to realise nothing lasts forever, so what do you have to lose? Why should you care so much about what people think of you? Why should you be so hard on yourself?

Use this knowledge to your advantage and let it give you new energy to accept and let go of negativity and disbelief. Make the most of this beautiful life you were gifted with. I remind myself of my mortality every morning, setting me up for a more accepting and grateful approach to the day. Try it!

THE FIVE BY FIVE RULE!

"If it won't matter in five years, don't waste more than five minutes worrying about it now."

Are you worrying about something that most probably won't be a big deal in the grand scheme of your life? Will it really matter in five years time? Then, it's not that important. Face the feelings about the situation, take a deep breath and move on. A great example is someone honking at you in traffic (e.g. the ugly toad guy). Will this incident matter in five years time? Probably not!

WHAT YOU RESIST, PERSISTS

Remind yourself of Carl Jung's quote when you find yourself wrestling with a difficult situation. *What you resist, persists, and what you accept you can change!*

It makes very little sense to give your energy and attention to situations which you don't want to see in your life. A good example is with the monk that tricked me out of my money. If I keep thinking about how I hate people stealing money from me, I will keep noticing similar situations going on around me. I might even attract a repeat of the situation as that's all I am feeding my mind. Since I'm resisting what happened, it will persist in my life. However, if I stop resisting and instead focus my mental energy on how much I love it when strangers smile at me, I will notice many more people smiling at me and each other. I will also attract people smiling at me much more because they will be able to pick up the kind of vibe I put out into this world. *"Common' crack a smile for this guy."*

Stop resisting things you don't want to see in your life, and start focusing on how you want your life to unfold.

LOOK IN THE MIRROR

I mentioned this step in the body of this chapter. You should aim to be looking in the mirror every single day. Not to check if your mono-brow is growing back but to look yourself in the eyes. Tell yourself you love and accept yourself how you are right now. You don't need to earn your right to be happy. You don't need to wait until you're with the perfect partner. It might feel slightly unusual at first and might even be difficult, but the mirror exercise is highly rewarding. Try it every day for 14 days and you'll feel an immense shift in your life. I recently recommended this technique to a friend who was having a hard time accepting herself after being rejected by a guy. She told me it was a game-changer, she's now happily travelling the world.

TRY OUT MBCT

Mindfulness-based cognitive therapy was developed for people who suffer from repeated spells of depression and chronic unhappiness. I think this teaching is useful for everyone. Often, we know that we should show more acceptance and love for ourselves but find it hard to put it into practise. Standing in front of a mirror is great but acceptance also goes deeper than that. MBCT teaches us how to become aware of sensation in our body (e.g. heavy shoulders when sad). With acceptance and learning to 'let it be', we can end the resistance and as we discovered, *what you resist, persist – what you accept you can change.* A large part of MBCT is mindfulness meditations, so if you carry out the mindfulness meditations we discussed in chapter three, you will already reap some of these benefits. If you want to go more in-depth and would like some guidance, it can certainly be worth taking an MBCT programme or researching the topic. The programme usually consists of eight weekly classes and a set of guided meditations to be carried out at home. You can find mental health professionals who are trained in delivering MBCT therapy in many countries across the world (now also in Martinique and South Korea!). Visit: https://www.accessmbct.com

The mindfulness wave is spreading!

Advanced Steps for Acceptance

SEE THE POSITIVE IN EVERY SITUATION

Spot the blessing in disguise. This step goes beyond accepting the situation as it is because you also attribute a positive value to it. This method is an advanced step because in practise, it can be difficult to draw out the positive. For example, those who suffer from a severe illness such as cancer. It can be hard to see the positive in life when you're faced with cancer, however research published in the *Journal of Happiness Studies* has shown that the link between unhappiness and illness is not so straightforward. We might think that those with the most severe illnesses are also the unhappiest but that's often not the case. People faced with severe illness often develop resilience. Many severely ill people I know are some of the happiest people I know. In other words, just because you were dealt difficult cards, it doesn't mean you can't focus on positive aspects of your life. If people facing severe illness can do it, surely you can do it too when faced with something far less severe?

I often view failed relationships or friendships in this light. Although it can hurt, the situation will have taught me a lesson about myself or the world that I still had to learn. I can only become wiser and stronger from it in the long run. Moreover, my illness was the biggest wake-up call. In hindsight, despite the suffering, it was also a positive experience because I became a person I might have never become otherwise. Happier, healthier and simply closer to my true self than ever before. When I was going through the hardship of not being able to get out of bed or feeling terrible with constant headaches, it was hard to find the positive in the situation. However, when I did focus on the positive, it completely shifted my mood. You accept all that is and let it be, and then draw your attention to the positive or valuable outcomes. In most cases, there is something. It could even help to get out pen and paper and see if something comes to mind.

TRULY LOVE YOURSELF

Focus on the in-depth feeling of cultivating love for yourself. Truly loving yourself. There are a range of strategies to develop more self-love, many of which you will have found in this chapter and will encounter throughout this book. Other resources include *You Are a Badass: How to Stop Doubting Your Greatness and Start Living an Awesome Life* by Jen Sincero which expands on self-love in a fun way! *How to Love Yourself: Cherishing the Incredible Miracle That You Are* by Louise Hay is also another great read. Highly rewarding, when you are ready.

IN A NUTSHELL

- Acceptance is important to manage and navigate through life effectively.

- In theory, if you can accept a situation, you can be happy.

- You have the choice. Resist and be unhappy or accept and be happy.

- When you blame external circumstances, the cycle of non-acceptance is never ending.

- Acceptance does not mean passively taking everything life throws at you like a slob, it means taking control of your response. Taking action to resolve issues that can be resolved still remains key.

- Acceptance means living a boss-like existence.

- Don't sweep it under the rug! Acceptance does not mean blanking out everything around you. Acceptance needs to work in partnership with facing everything that arises.

- We should try saying 'F**k it' more often (gentler alternatives are allowed too).

- What you resist, persists. What you accept, you can change.

- Loving yourself unconditionally is the next level of acceptance and a lifelong job. It's highly rewarding, however.
- Acceptance will make you more confident.
- Acceptance will become your (slightly addictive) super-power.
- Most importantly, don't trust every monk you meet!

SUMMARY OF STEPS

1. Use a Phrase to Zap You into Acceptance Mode
2. Make Acceptance A Life Goal
3. Use the Outsider's View
4. Be Kind to Yourself. Forgive Yourself
5. Remind Yourself of Your Mortality
6. The Five by Five Rule!
7. What You Resist, Persists
8. Look in the Mirror
9. Try out MBCT

ADVANCED STEPS

- See the Positive in Every Situation
- Truly Love Yourself

Want to know a nice side effect of becoming more accepting?

You will become the embodiment of confidence.

Maybe not straight away, but with time, you will! When you accept yourself and your situation, your self-esteem increases, and you start to become more self-confident. True confidence isn't based on the absence of fear, but the presence of love. Increased self-confidence means that you will trust your ability to achieve whatever you set out to do. What's not to love about that?

CHAPTER 5: GRATITUDE

"The secret of happiness is to count your blessings while others are adding up their troubles."

William Penn (English Nobleman)

Gratitude is one of my favourite parts of my Happiness Button, and a vital ingredient. If you only increase gratitude in your life, you will already massively increase your happiness. However, gratitude is rare. We only feel a strong sense of gratitude when something comes along to threaten life as we know it.

When we watch the news, we become sad and compassionate for those living in troubled areas of the world, and it might make us feel grateful for living in peace. Why do we need to be exposed to these horrible scenarios to feel grateful? How often are we randomly appreciative of being alive, having our health, having food and living in peace?

I've worked with disabled students for a few years now, and it really has made me more grateful. I'm grateful for everything I'm able to do. After working with blind students, I'm particularly grateful for being able to see the world around me. My body performs so many complex tasks daily, and I'm incredibly grateful for it all. Why was I not grateful to start off with? Why isn't gratitude our default setting?

Often, we are too occupied and focused on what we *don't* have in our lives, that we overlook what we do. From an evolutionary standpoint, it's a survival mechanism to shift our focus to accumulating more so we can be the strongest and most prepared for tough times. The problem is that our lack of gratitude for what we *do* have impedes our well-being today! We're making ourselves unhappy when there's no need to be. Especially as living standards have raised and we don't need to fight each other for the last piece of bread (unless it's Black Friday).

We are too often in a mindset of *scarcity* which makes us blind to all the fantastic things we have in life. The things we *don't* have, simply pull too vigorously for our attention.

Legendary entrepreneur and social media guru Gary Vaynerchuk, doesn't preach how to triple your income but instead, how to be more grateful. He claims to be a very happy man because of it. He writes that he's sick of the 'glass half empty' analogy as most people's glasses are four-fifths full and he's grateful for just one drop in the glass (because he knows how to invest it!).

On the topic of Americans, they have a national holiday to practise gratitude. What's it called? Ah yes, Thanksgiving! How grateful are people really on this day? Are they more concerned with stuffing the perfect Turkey, making gravy and arguing with family members? (No offence my US friends, that's just an outsider's perspective). I propose that we have our own unofficial Thanksgiving every single day, minus the turkey and arguing.

Gratitude Changed My Life

When I was ill, all I wanted was to be better and live a normal life. I wanted to spend time with my friends, have enough energy, get a job and make money. I suffered under the things I couldn't do and didn't have. After I started to get better, I didn't find my thoughts about wanting things or lacking things going away. My health was improving but I had missed out on 3 to 4 years of 'living'. Now, there were new things to want and worry about.

The mind and ego will always supply us with reasons why our life is not good enough, even when we are objectively doing much better than the past. The solution is very straightforward;

You have to become satisfied and content with what you have in life right now. Don't let never-ending desire rule you.

Although I couldn't socialise much, felt left behind and didn't have much energy, I *did* have a place to stay, food, and most of my other physical and mental health. Studies have shown that gratitude can strengthen the immune system. This is mostly because gratitude reduces stress and makes you feel at ease. Stress is a real troublemaker in the body, it's good to keep it at bay! I have no doubt that gratitude greatly contributed to overcoming my illness.

Gratitude Is Not Just About You

Adopting a grateful mindset is not only about increasing your own happiness, but also about recognising we are part of larger relationship with the world around us. To function, gratitude needs to be reciprocal in nature (receiving and giving!). I know way too many people who only want to take, take, take and then they're surprised when no one is there to listen or help them.

Many philosophers have even suggested that gratitude is the glue holding us all together. Even Adam Smith, the economist dude who preached self-interest, argued that gratitude is key for social stability! Although the cohesion of society depends on a range of factors, I do think there is a lot of truth to attributing some of this to gratitude. If we can increase gratitude on an individual level, society as a whole should become more stable and functional.

Abundance vs. Scarcity

Abundance: The feeling of having more than enough.

Scarcity: The feeling of lacking something or not having enough of something. *I don't have enough of this... I don't have enough of that... I'm not good enough... I wish I had... I wish I was more like...*

True and sustained happiness is not possible when you are in a mindset of scarcity. You will be chasing hits of happiness to trick you into feeling that you have enough. Before long, that feeling of fulfilment evaporates into nothingness.

You need to be in a mindset of abundance, and gratitude gets you there. <u>Your state of mind is separate from your circumstances</u>. What does that mean? It means you don't need to be a millionaire to feel like you have more than enough! It all depends how you look at it.

That being said, it will be a lot easier to practise gratitude when you are not caught up in an intense struggle for survival. What you *shouldn't* do is settle in miserable circumstances and tell yourself you are in abundance. Your mind will most likely have a hard time believing you. Keep reaching to make life easier and better for yourself. Don't fall into the scarcity trap.

Scarcity vs. Abundance in A Real Life Scenario

It's 5pm. You've finished work for the day and head home. Your friend is already waiting for you outside your house like a well-trained puppy, ready to go for a stroll around the neighbourhood. You feel the warm summer breeze wiping away some of the stresses of the day. You turn a corner. No, you don't see a thug monk but a huge and newly renovated house. It's remarkably modern and stylish. Possibly inspired by Le Corbusier. You both look at the house and then look at each other. You agree how great it would be to have a home like that one day. Imagine all the space you'd have. The kitchen surely has marble worktops: you've always dreamed of having marble worktops. For the rest of the walk, you think about how much your apartment sucks compared to this amazing house. You can't let go of it. Every morning on your way to work, you drive past the newly renovated house and the same thought enters your mind. *Man, when I have a house like that, I'll be much happier. My place sucks big time.* That's scarcity in its purest form, the feeling of lack makes you unhappy.

Abundance shines a different light on the same situation.

One week later, you pass the beautiful big house again. This time a homeless man is making his way down the street, carrying all his belongings in two plastic bags. A thought pops into your head. *Man, I bet this homeless guy would be so happy to live in my apartment. Even if just for a week. It would mean shelter, safety, and food.* You think about how lucky and blessed you are to have a place to live. You don't need to worry about getting kicked out or having people rob you in your sleep. You notice the newly renovated house behind the homeless man. You appreciate the look of it and that's where the thought ends. There's no urgency to move because you're already in a state of abundance. You can't have more than more than enough.

Most people are stuck in the scarcity mindset, and that's why their situation rarely changes. My clothing line Gratitude=Abundance is here to remind us of this important mindset! Being grateful for what you have (which is plenty) takes you to a state of abundance. Nothing spreads good vibes and makes people think more than a big fat GRATITUDE=ABUNDANCE print on the front of a t-shirt, hoodie or mug! You can find the clothing line in the shop on my website (https://felixnew.com/shop).

Steps to Happiness via Gratitude

KEEP A GRATITUDE JOURNAL

Yes, I know what some of you might say. *Journal?! I don't do journals. That's just not me.* Einstein, Darwin, Marie Curi, Richard Branson, Leonardo Da Vinci, Oprah Winfrey, John D. Rockefeller and many more legendary people all kept or keep a journal, and they didn't do too badly in life, right?

Keeping a gratitude journal does not take any time at all. Two to five minutes in the morning and two to five minutes before you sleep. By just investing up to 10 minutes a day, you'll substantially improve your life for the better.

No matter how much we pretend to cope with everything ourselves, writing things down supports your well-being. It makes you feel heard. I used to take pride in being able to deal with life's struggles by myself but just like everyone else, I'm in need of a listening ear from time to time. Writing helped with that. It's free therapy. Writing also makes you more committed to what you scribble down. When you write *I'm grateful for Oreo cookies,* you'll most likely be more grateful the next time you pick one up.

In the morning, your mind is still fresh and hasn't yet been compromised by a flurry of negative thoughts. When you whip out the gratitude journal, you immediately divert your mind to more abundant, positive thinking. It's a good alternative to checking your phone which is more of an accomplishment drainer. At night, it calms your mind and allows you to reflect on the day.

Keeping a gratitude journal has a serious knock-on effect.

The beautiful thing about keeping a gratitude journal is that you'll start to spot things in everyday life you're grateful for. No matter how your day has gone. It's almost like a magnet attracting more and more feelings of gratitude. Gratitude=Abundance.

How should I use my gratitude journal?

There are a few points that I write down and repeat to myself every morning and every night. Other points depend on what I feel grateful for in that particular moment.

I am grateful for being alive (This is key for me - when you are grateful for simply being alive, you instantly feel happier).

I am grateful for my mental and physical well-being

I am grateful for the roof over my head and the food I have

I am grateful for having friends and family in my life

I am grateful for the peace around me (no war)

GO ON GRATITUDE WALKS

Gratitude walks are super easy to incorporate into your daily life. While walking, bring to mind the things you are grateful for or bring to mind what you feel you should be more grateful for. Think about each topic in some detail and start to feel a deep sense of gratitude within yourself.

Why can't I do this from my comfy sofa?

- Walking puts you in a fresh environment which will bring about a refreshing change in your thinking.

- Walking outside gives your brain oxygen to think clearly. The outside environment will stimulate your senses.

- There is nothing quite like feeling the fresh air on your face and your feet moving on the ground. Try to find a green spot somewhere, it will be worth the walk! If you're feeling up to it, try to see the beauty exactly where you are.

- *All truly great thoughts are conceived by walking* (Friedrich Nietzsche)

I would suggest taking gratitude walks by yourself, so you don't get distracted or caught up. For me, gratitude walks are a somewhat personal thing. Felix New time.

GET RID OF THE COMPARING MIND

"Comparison is the thief of joy."
Theodore Roosevelt

Your Comparison is Unjust

Your judgement is unfair, and a perfect example is social media. It might make you feel bad seeing friends post exotic happy holiday photos. What you forget is that for the other 350 days of the year, their reality does not reflect a tropical holiday. They might be far more miserable than people imagine. Everyone has their problems even when they're swimming in money or travelling the world. Also, you will often be comparing your weakness with someone else's strength. Sure, Novak Djokovic is much better at tennis than you are but you're a better singer or cook than him or whatever your strength may be! Did you know there's a video of Novak Djokovic singing *Call Me Maybe*? I don't recommend you watch it.

You Are Unique

You can't compare a water bottle to a kettle. They work in different ways and have a different purpose on this planet. It's the same for you and me. I used to feel down when I compared myself to some musical artists. *How will I ever hit notes like that or write those melodies? I sound more like a red fox howling when I attempt those notes.* Focusing on my uniqueness helped to solve this problem. I might not be able to sing as pitch-perfect as them but I am perfect at pouring my own style and heart into songs. If Beyoncé tried to be like Felix New, she would also start to doubt herself.

Focus on Celebrating Yourself Along the Way

The only person you should compare yourself with is yourself. Congratulate yourself for achievements you make along the way. Congratulate yourself for becoming the best version of yourself or doing something better than you would have done in the past. That's how you grow. That's how you become happy and grateful with who you are.

Be Inspired by Others, Not Jealous!

Think back to the last time you felt a sense of jealousy, could you shift your mindset instead to look at this person as inspiration? Try it! When you look at others through this lens, your life will transform for the better.

Focus on Things You Can't Buy

To some degree, you can compare wealth and success, but you certainly can't compare love and all the other amazing inter-human qualities. Focus on cultivating these qualities, and you will automatically reduce your comparing mind.

PLACE VISUAL REMINDERS IN YOUR ENVIRONMENT

When life gets busy, we often forget to be grateful. That's why we need reminders to snap us back into gratitude mode. For me, I always see my Gratitude=Abundance hoodie in my room or on my body, so that helps. Now that I am writing, I realise that I don't have too many visual reminders for when I'm on-the-go. Our cities are not exactly filled with reminders to be grateful. There's certainly room to implement something new! Do you have any ideas? Let me know in the *My Happiness Button* Facebook group or drop me an email.

BE GRATEFUL FOR YOUR CHALLENGES

Have your past or current challenges turned you into a better person? Are you now healthier, tougher, smarter, more compassionate? As tough as they may have been, they have most likely helped you grow. Be grateful for them.

VOLUNTEER

Volunteering will make you more grateful and compassionate. It will remind you of the blessings you have in life. Seeing how other people live their lives will put things into perspective. I volunteered at a mental health community centre a few years ago, and it elevated my gratitude level greatly. Get out there and level up your gratitude by volunteering.

PRAYER AND GRATITUDE MEDITATIONS

Be sure to incorporate prayers of gratitude into your day if it aligns with your beliefs.

Meditation can help you level up your gratitude game and help to re-shape your mind to become more grateful. Buddhist monks start their day with a chant of gratitude and Native American elders start each ceremony with gratitude for the earth, sky and plants which sustain them. Essentially, these meditations are about bringing to mind all you're grateful for and meditating on it. It's an enriching way for your mind to soak up your intentions, thus leaving you more grateful as you go through your day. With continued practise, you'll harvest much gratitude.

SPEAK LIKE A GRATEFUL PERSON

Grateful people have a certain way of expressing themselves. They don't use phrases that make them seem like a victim of their circumstances. Such as *why always me, why can't I have… Urgh this is always so stupid.* Instead, they use words that show their attitude of gratitude, acceptance and self-control. *I'm thankful for this opportunity. Many aspects of this are fantastic.* Try to choose phrases that make it easier to remain grateful.

WRITE LETTERS OF GRATITUDE TO FRIENDS, FAMILY AND STRANGERS

Show your appreciation for others with a small note or letter. Writing down your gratitude solidifies the grateful thoughts. A friend of mine does this all the time and oh my, does it produce many smiles on others faces and not to forget her own. Besides, who still writes letters tzhese days? You'll get extra brownie points for it!

The great thing about gratitude is that you don't need to learn many techniques. Deep down, you know how to be grateful. You might need some time to make it a daily practise in your life, but this will become increasingly easier for you.

A Happiness Button Exercise

Write down three things you are grateful for in your life. How does it feel?

Now take another piece of paper and write down three things you appreciate about someone in your life. Give it to them. How does it feel? How did they respond?

Now you've started the process of journaling. Keep doing it. Harvest that gratitude and spread it to others!

IN A NUTSHELL

- Increase gratitude in your life to increase your happiness.

- Often, we are only reminded to be grateful when we lose something (e.g. health).

- Be happy for what you *do* have in your life.

- A scarcity mindset keeps you stuck in unhappiness.

- Gratitude is a direct path to abundance.

- Your state of mind is separate from your circumstances. You don't need to be a millionaire to be grateful for the wealth in your life.

- Gratitude is not just about you. It also helps spread good in the world.
- Philosophers have suggested that gratitude is the glue holding us all together.
- You don't need to learn anything to get started, you can practise gratitude right now (Try the Happiness Button Exercise).

SUMMARY OF THE STEPS

1. Keep a Gratitude Journal
2. Go on Gratitude Walks
3. Get Rid of the Comparing Mind
4. Place Visual Reminders in Your Environment
5. Be Grateful for Your Challenges
6. Volunteer
7. Prayer and Gratitude Meditation
8. Speak Like a Grateful Person
9. Write Letters of Gratitude to Friends, Family and Strangers

ADDITIONAL RESOURCES

Gratitude Journaling - What Do I Use?

A lot of people use either a simple sheet of paper or the *5-Minute Journal*.

Alex Ikonn, the co-founder of the *5-Minute-Journal* describes it as '*a toothbrush for the mind*'. Ideally, you do it day and night. There is even an app for *the 5-minute journal* but I'm more of a paper guy. How about you?

On my website, you can download a free weekly gratitude journal I have arranged for you (www.felixnew.com). *365 Gratitude Journal* is a free resource you can use and track your days on the calendar view. This app could become a good friend of yours. The point is, it doesn't matter what you use! You could even write on the tissues of your favourite fast-food store if it works for you. Just make sure to write down what you're grateful for once in the morning and once at night. Every day.

Advanced: Sometimes I simply bring things to mind and 'mentally journal'. This can work fine and still bring you benefits. If I'm in a rush in the morning, I mentally journal the way to my destination. However, try to write it down when possible as this has proven to be more effective. Another benefit of writing down what you are grateful for is that you can look back at what you wrote and do more of this specific thing to make you feel abundant and on top of the world!

Gratitude Meditation – What Do I Use?

Jack Kornfield, who has been teaching meditation classes since 1974 and who has been a key to bringing Buddhist mindfulness concepts to the western world, shares some beautiful words on gratitude meditations on his website. https://jackkornfield.com/meditation-gratitude-joy/. You can find gratitude meditations on Jack's website or also in the *Insight Timer* app.

A stinking rich entrepreneur created another fantastic gratitude meditation I use. The man goes by the name of Dan Lok. Look him up, he has quite the story to tell! The idea might not sound awfully spiritual to you right now but for me, Dan Lok has the perfect mix of 'stop messing about' and 'your life is a blessing' in this meditation. I even shed a tear when I first did the meditation because I felt so grateful and at peace. Find it on *YouTube* by searching *Guided Meditation on Gratitude – 15-Minute-Miracle Exercise*. More and more successful people in business are realising the benefit of gratitude and meditation in general!

CHAPTER 6: AFFIRMATIONS

"An affirmation opens the door. It's a beginning point on the path to change."

Louise L. Hay

Affirmations are positive statements repeated to yourself in order to challenge the impact of negative thoughts. They influence your conscious and unconscious mind to turn you into a positive and powerful human being! As you repeat positive statements to yourself consistently, you are motivated to change your behaviour, and become aligned with these statements. Make your unconscious work *for* you and not *against* you.

To understand affirmations better, the term *fake it 'till you make it* is useful. This is also known as *act as if* among life coaches and personal development folk. The idea is simple: bring to mind qualities you feel you lack but would like to have such as confidence or competence. Then, *act as if* you embody these qualities in real life. You make these qualities become your REALITY by changing your behaviour to change the way you feel. This is crucially important because most of us are overly critically of our abilities (remember the inner critic).

An overwhelming number of people swear by this method for becoming successful, using *act as if*, author of the #1 NY Times bestselling book *Secrets of the Millionaire Mind*, T. Harv Eker became a millionaire in only two and a half years. If you'd like to know more, psychologist and bestselling author, Richard Wiseman has written a book called the *As if Principle*. Furthermore, Harvard professor Amy Cuddy's TED Talk reached over 13 million people online when she crucially explained that you shouldn't just *fake it 'till you make it*, but rather *fake it 'till you become it*. In other words, you should keep going until you have reached a point where you've managed to internalise whatever it is you've been affirming. This notion can be wonderfully illustrated by popular author, Paulo Coehlo.

> *"You must be the person you have never had the courage to be.*
> *Gradually, you will discover that you are that person, but until you can see this clearly, you must pretend and invent."*
>
> Paulo Coelho

Do Affirmations Work or Are They Just Wishful Thinking?

If I were answering this question before my transformation to my healthier, wealthier and happier self, I would have said: *No, affirmations don't work! Don't be ridiculous. You can't simply wish for something and then have it turn up. Life isn't that easy.*

However, affirmations have worked very well in different areas of my life. Ever since Teletubbies was still airing on TV, I've always been somewhat of a shy guy. I've never been a fan of being the centre of attention, and I've always been afraid of public speaking. Speaking to one person was fine, I've never been extremely shy but add more than two people and I would go silent. I still remember getting sweaty hands and going bright red in almost every class presentation. I hated hearing my voice become more and more high pitched and feeling my hands trembling as my voice was the only noise filling the room. It was almost torturous. University was a little better, but I was still not over it.

I learned about affirmations in the book *The Miracle Morning* by Hal Elrod. It was crystal clear to me what my first affirmation had to be. I would affirm confidence.

I would write down and say out loud: *I am truly confident. I am truly a confident person in any possible situation.*

I affirmed this sentence in the morning and before going to sleep at night. I would often imagine myself in

Felix New's tip for confidence:

For a feeling of self–worth and confidence in your abilities, it's equally important to mark small continuous successes. These successes prove to yourself that you are capable. If you're scared of talking to strangers, talk to a stranger a day and feel your confidence grow over time. Every morning write on a sheet of paper: 'I will talk to a stranger today'. Then tick it off once you've done it. You'll have hard evidence for why you should feel confident!

situations and repeat the phrase. *I am truly confident in the meeting at work today. I am truly confident when I meet my friends. I am truly confident when I am at the shop. I am truly confident in the test today.* In my vision, I was known as the most confident guy in town. At first, I could not convince my mind to believe I was a confident superhuman. The memories and voices of the past were too noisy and kept creeping back in. *'No, you're not confident, it doesn't matter if you keep saying it. Too many situations still scare the hell out of you! You're just as easily scared as a damn chicken'.*

Despite an initial resistance, my affirmations were working. Whenever I faced situations where I felt shy or scared, I would bring the affirmation to mind. It would make me a little less scared and a little more confident. I could feel my general level of confidence growing. I could hold eye contact longer. Friends would mention that they noticed I had become more decisive and funny. People started treating me differently. I felt more respected. I started to become the person I imagined in my vision for so long. I acted *as if* to become who I wished to be.

Even today, I still do the affirmation every single day. It's a process and a long-term project, not a quick fix but with the right mindset, you learn to run directly at fear and rise above it in the process. If you also struggle with confidence, this method might just work wonders for you. You'll turn negative self-talk into positive self-talk. Of course, it's not the only component to developing confidence but it's very effective when practised consistently.

Aff-normations

If you don't phrase your affirmations correctly, they might not work. Your unconscious might end up working against you instead.

There is a great YouTube channel run by Gavin Stephenson called *Wake Up Fulfilled*. After digging deep to discover his true purpose, he became an expert on self-development and aff-normations. *Don't you mean affirmations, Felix?* Nope, I mean aff-normations.

Although *act as if* affirmations can be effective for some, it can also be useful to ditch them. Gavin claims that we should be 'normalising' our experience instead. *It's normal for me to be confident or It's normal for me to be happy.* If it's normal for you, the focus is less on what you don't have yet. Your inner critic finds it harder to attack what is 'normal' for you.

We can also use our body to help us! We can shrug our shoulders while we say *it's normal for me to be happy.* By shrugging those shoulders, you enforce the feeling that being happy is a state of mind you normally gravitate towards and possess by default. Get creative, use gestures in front of the mirror - whatever helps you normalise what you affirm and wish to see in your life. The idea of normalising is an interesting approach we can use to fine-tune our affirmations. I suggest that you try both affirmation and aff-normations.

Why do Some People Still Insist that Affirmations Don't Work?

If you're familiar with self-development, you'll know that although affirmations are hugely popular, they are also not loved by everyone. After telling a good friend of mine about the benefits of affirmations, he said to me, '*Felix, affirmations are nothing more than wishful thinking. I don't mean to offend you but it's slightly delusional. How can I get myself to believe things that are not true? Wouldn't I just be lying to myself?*'

I swiftly replied, '*John, my dear friend. When a physically unfit person thinks he can run a half marathon in a decent time without any training, some might also call that delusional. This is why they train to become fit and improve their physical health. Affirmations are no different, only in that they train your mind. You repeatedly exercise your mind by practising positive thoughts. Just like the runner starts to lose fat and gain muscle, the person practising affirmations starts to reduce negative thoughts and increase positive ones. The more the runner trains, the fitter he becomes. The more the affirmator affirms, the more positive his thoughts and life will become.*

More positive thoughts result in more positive actions. If you only think in terms of what your mind perceives as 'realistic', this will never make you happy or successful. Your ego will make you believe you are not good enough. Don't listen to the inner critic. Be a little delusional if you have to. That's okay. It's better than being unhappy and unsuccessful. When used to affirm positive action, affirmations change your *can't do* attitude to a *can do* attitude.

> *"Those who think they can and those who think they can't are both usually right."*
>
> **Confucius (Chinese teacher)**

The Science Behind Affirmations

Did you know that you don't have the same brain you once did?

What? Are you saying someone has replaced it, Felix?

Of course, not! As we go through life, our brains change in response to what we are exposed to. This is known as neuroplasticity. That's why good parenting and a safe environment is so important for kids growing up. What we consume mentally changes the physiology of our brains over time. When positive affirmations are repeated or consumed consistently, this can establish new neural connections that alter the physiology of your brain. Isn't that incredible?

Let's say you always affirm yourself that drinking tea makes you happy. Pathways in your brain will start to associate tea with feeling good and thus, you will be more likely to seek out new opportunities to get your hands on tea. This is the exact reason why companies spend millions on advertising

Now imagine you replace tea with getting up early in the morning or going outside your comfort zone at social events. Repetition, repetition, repetition, repetition is key. With repetition, new pathways are formed. You change your mind and behaviour most powerfully with affirmations, so treat this power with care!

> *"With great power comes great responsibility."*
> **Uncle Ben/Spiderman**

Professor Christopher Cascio and his colleagues had a look at what goes on inside our brains when we use affirmations. They put study participants into an fMRI scanner, a big noisy machine that looks like a doughnut and scans your brain The study found that regions of the brain responsible for positive self-valuation showed increased activity in those who practised affirmations. There was a clear relationship between the use of reward pathways in the brain and affirmations; the big doughnut scanner picked up on it.

Researchers think a key reason why affirmations work is because they make you see beyond a given threat. For me, presentations at school seemed like a real threat. However, with affirmations I was able to see beyond it. They broaden your perspective to make you see the brighter side of life and not just this negative threat (not a Monty Python reference). In such instances, affirmations will undoubtedly make you happier. Even the wise Aristotle recognised the power of affirmations, as he argued that to become virtuous, one must first act as a virtuous person would. To keep it short and sweet, researchers have found that affirmations can make you less stressed, more focused, get better results in life and improve your overall well-being.

However, there is a problem when it comes to this ability to trick your mind, it goes by the name of 'negative self-talk'. Statistics tell us that we have between 50,000 to 70,000 thoughts every single day and 80% of these are supposedly negative. With this ability to brainwash yourself, you need to take extreme care when doing so. You need to devote increased effort to replace the negative self-talk that's making you unhappy, with positive self-talk that will make you happy! When you keep telling yourself you will fail at something, you most likely will fail. Confucius said, *"Those who think they can and those who think they can't are both usually right."* Your mind only reproduces what you feed it.

Any More Real Life Examples?

I came across a comment on a YouTube video that blew my mind. I knew affirmations were powerful from my own life and that of friends and people I've helped, but when you're faced with intense real life stories from strangers, that's something else.

Anonymous Affirmator – A year ago, I had three people who were dependent on me for income. At the same time, I was struggling with a drug addiction, and desperately trying to become clean. It was the moment that I was feeling extremely anxious about how to feed my family and how to pay rent that I ended up on an affirmation video. Something clicked for me instantly. If it was working for other people, I had to try it too – I had nothing to lose. I came up with the following affirmations that I would repeat day and night. "I deserve to be financially stable", "I am in the process of changing my life", "My life and income is improving".

It wasn't long before I started to see real change in my life. A friend asked me to join his business, and before I knew it, I was making more money than I had ever made before. I truly became a better person in the process. Others would tell me how positive I've become and I couldn't help but to do all I could for those who need help. I've stopped using drugs. My family is financially stable. We are planning a family holiday soon. Affirmations are nothing short from lifesavers.

Felix New's eight daily affirmations

1. I am truly happy. I truly feel happiness flowing through my body all day (or it is normal for me to be truly happy).

2. I am truly confident. I am a truly confident person in any possible situation (or it is normal for me to be truly confident).

3. I truly take action all day, making the most of this life (or it is normal for me to truly take action, making the most of this life).

4. I truly have money in abundance (or it is normal for me to truly have money in abundance).

5. I truly have deep and meaningful relationships with my family and friends (or it is normal for me to have deep and meaningful relationships with my family and friends).

6. I am truly a successful author of the book *My Happiness Button* which helps people live happier lives. (or it is normal for me…).

7. I am truly fit and healthy. I exercise at least three times a week and I choose to eat healthy. (or it is normal for me…).

8. I am truly destined for greatness. (or it is normal for me…).

The content of my affirmations changes from time to time to adapt to my current situation but my commitment to them doesn't change. I write them down or say them out loud every day. Mornings are key to set your intentions for the day, a day filled with positivity, joy, confidence, and love. Affirmations also send you to sleep peacefully at night, knowing you are moving closer to the person you wish to become. A perfect way to start and end your day.

What Kind of Affirmations Can I Set?

Affirmations are statements about *what you* want in your life, so they can be whateve*r you* want! Seriously. Apart from being able to fly or something absurd and virtually impossible. You obviously can't turn into an eight-legged rhinoceros, okay?

Key Factors for Making Affirmations Work

It's strikingly important to connect with what you are saying. Ask yourself how much you want to change your life. How badly do you want these affirmations to become reality? Realise how meaningful these affirmations are. Why did you choose them? If they are no longer meaningful, then change them to something that is!

- ## Use Visualisations

When you affirm, make sure you truly imagine yourself in the situation. What will it feel like to be where you want to be? What emotions will you feel? Visualising will make it all the more real and your conscious, as well as your unconscious mind, will start taking your affirmations seriously. Make it sensory and as rich as possible. Visualise what it will feel like to be happy. Visualise the overall positive feeling carrying you through your day, and your unshakable feeling of tranquillity.

- ## Make Your Affirmations Believable

Keep in mind when choosing your affirmations that they can't be too unrealistic or else you risk your mind rejecting them. My friend 'John' did make a fair point, there *is* only a certain level of delusion that your mind is willing to accept. I suggest you experiment with this to see where your limits are.

- ## Be Exact in Your Wording

You're going to need some detail. For some people, affirmations like *I will be wealthy* are too vague. What helped me was telling myself *I will earn X amount by April 2019 by seeking out new opportunities and making the most out of my current ones.* Being specific makes sure you have laser focus on your vision and therefore reduces the risk of confusing your mind. You can't really put a number on happiness, but you can still be specific about how you envision you will feel and what your life will be like.

- **Experiment with Different Types of Affirmations**

The study by Cascio and his colleagues found that basing affirmations on the future is the most effective way to practise them. What type of affirmations work best depends on the individual. For some people, it's more useful to talk about what they *will* have instead of what they have. They feel that it's a motivating push to work towards their dream life. It's all about establishing what works best for you.

The Law of Attraction

Affirmations are often used by people who believe in 'the law of attraction'. A famous book you might have heard of, *The Secret* by Rhonda Byrne, was the catalyst that turned the law of attraction (and affirmations) into a big topic of discussion. The book has sold over 20 million copies and has been translated into 50 languages. You can safely say that people have heard of it. While I know some people who take it a little far, the law of attraction can be highly beneficial to our lives if we understand its nature.

What does the law of attraction say?

Everything that happens to you is brought into your life because of your thoughts and resulting energy. *Like attracts like.* This means, for example, that if you keep thinking undesirable thoughts, you will keep attracting undesirable things. In order to attain what you desire, you must first feel that the desired outcome has already occurred. If there's something you want to manifest (a word law of attraction users LOVE) something into your life, you need to have a *clear* vision and a *clear* plan to receive what you desire. It's key for you to visualise and feel as if the outcome has already occurred in your life via affirmations. Importantly, many people who subscribe to the law of attraction believe that if the frequencies you send out are unclear, then you will not receive the desired outcome. If you only partly want to feel happy then you will most probably not feel better as a result of your affirmations. You need to be clear and sure of what you are requesting.

The law of attraction used to confuse me and seem like a scam. These days, it makes a lot of sense to me. When you affirm your affirmations (what a sentence!), your mind starts to focus on what you are feeding it and then takes action consciously and unconsciously to get there. The law of attraction works because our minds always try to find solutions to the problems in our life. Our minds solve problems, that's what they do.

There's also another key ingredient that's often missed when people talk about the law of attraction. If you take away the first four letters of the word *attraction*, then what do you get? **ACTION!** Some people believe that you just need to think about becoming richer, happier or landing a dream job and you will achieve it. Of course, thinking about it will help but in order to achieve anything in life, you need to also take deliberate consistent action. Meditate, volunteer, apply to jobs instead of watching TV, network with people, talk to strangers, practise gratitude. Without this type of action, you won't see the desired results.

Want something? Then affirm it, visualise it, take as much deliberate action towards it as possible and you will receive it. It's not magic, it's simply a way of explaining a process of attaining what you desire in your life.

Affirmations Are Cool – But Where Does Happiness Come In?

I know you picked up this book to learn about happiness, and so far this chapter has seemed like I'm trying to turn you into a rich business mogul. Yes, affirmations are most often used by people who wish to generate more wealth or popularity in their lives. A great example is Lady Gaga, who repeated the mantra *Music is my life, the fame is inside of me, I'm going to make a number one record* before she ever made it big in the music industry. Before she knew it, she was at the MTV Video Music Awards wearing a dress made entirely of raw beef.

The ability to affirm yourself is hugely important in a world that expects everything to happen instantly. There is so much happiness that we receive as a by-product of getting out there and making things happen, and many people require a sense of progress and purpose in order to feel happy. However, affirmations make you feel at ease, however good or bad you're doing. There's nothing better for your self-worth than telling yourself *I am destined for greatness, it's normal for me to be great* (even if you are far from it). With affirmations on your side, you can take some weight off your shoulders and see beyond the 'threat'.

Whenever I affirm happiness, I feel happier. I can feel a wave of happiness carrying me through my day. If I'm in a bad mood, it always gets better with affirmations. I also feel that my mind has started to believe that it's normal for me to be happy. Affirming happiness is similar to putting on a smile, even when you don't feel like it. *Were you ever in a terrible mood and then someone made you smile, and you couldn't help but feel better?* When you smile you instantly feel better. That's why we resort to cute cat videos to cheer us up. You always smile when watching cute cats. It's your bodies response connected with the physical sensation of smiling. It works in a very similar way with affirming happiness.

Many of my affirmations make me happier. My example of becoming more confident illustrates that as increased confidence tackled a key source of suffering in my life. It made it easier for me to accept who I am and love myself. Some people even believe that confidence is the root of happiness.

It's hard to outsmart our human nature. Negative thinking is a way of protecting ourselves (although a very ineffective one most of the time!) To survive, your mind finds all that is wrong in order to prepare and protect itself against danger. Does this sound familiar? (Okay, the next example might be based on me). You show your friends a song you wrote. If nine out of ten people tell you it's amazing and one person tells you that it's bad, you won't keep thinking about the nine positive comments. You'll focus on the one that was negative. Your mind is driven towards the 'threat' and tries to minimise any danger you might be facing. In your mind, that one negative comment is endangering your happiness and survival. It makes sense in theory but very little sense in practise. Why can't you enjoy the fact that 90% of people liked what you've done? Why do you have to pay one person so much of your precious mental energy and attention? This is where affirmations are extremely handy.

All these moments when you use affirmations do add up, and they help to work against the inner critic and negative thoughts that would otherwise take its place. It's an extremely useful tool to have in our toolbox as it can help switch your mindset and flood you with good vibes. To sum up, happiness is of course not attained simply by affirmations, but happiness based affirmations have proven to be a great way to enhance my mood and reprogram my mind to think more positively.

A Few Words of Caution...

I like to keep it real. As you saw from the example of the anonymous YouTube commenter, and my own example of increasing my confidence, affirmations can have huge positive value. However, just as with meditation, there is a chance that affirmations don't work for you. In most cases future based affirmations were found to work, so maybe stick with those first if you're finding affirmations a bit difficult.

Try writing down things you value, like your family or hobbies. There is a lot of research indicating that this kind of exercises has a positive affirming effect. It also places less focus on you as an individual. *My family will be happy and healthy, or it is normal for my family to be happy and healthy.* For most of you, affirmations will work and will be life-changing. Please drop me an e-mail with your results, I'm excited to hear what happens!

Take a moment right now to reflect if you feel that you need to. Put the book down, take a deep breath and process the information. Come back to the book when you are ready.

Are You Ready to Affirm Like There's No Tomorrow?!

I get it, affirmations are probably the most unusual step in this book. What will your friends and family think if they hear you chanting, *I am destined for greatness!* They'll probably think you've officially lost touch with reality. However, unusual doesn't mean ineffective. It's a very small commitment for the benefits you receive in return. It'll take you 10 minutes a day at most. To make life easier for you and to make sure you stick to it, you can download a free affirmation journal at felixnew.com. Otherwise, a notepad or a small journal works just as well.

Steps to Happiness via Affirmations

WHAT AREAS OF YOUR LIFE COULD BENEFIT FROM AFFIRMATIONS?

Keep a list of the things you want to improve on and things you want to dispel. Write down whenever a negative self-belief pops into your head and write down when you feel joy about something. Be sure to think of affirmations you can use to tackle or enhance these thoughts.

WHAT AFFIRMATIONS WORK FOR YOU?

Try different types of affirmations and see which ones work for you. Update your list of affirmations accordingly. Experiment which type of affirmations resonate most with you. Get rid of the ones you feel are not working. Use between one to ten affirmations at once. Anything beyond that will be confusing and less focused.

REPEAT YOUR AFFIRMATIONS DAILY

Knowing what you'll affirm is only half of the deal, you need to also stick to them. Write down your affirmations in the morning and at night. If writing is not your thing, then say them aloud or repeat them in your head when commuting to work. Your mind will start to internalise your affirmations as you repeat the process over, and over again. Keep repeating this cycle. Watch your affirmations become reality over time.

You can also use apps such as *The Affirmation Reminder* or *Spirit Junkie* which let you manage your affirmations and set reminders on your phone.

GET TO ZERO FIRST

If you are currently in the more negative realm of thinking, it can be a good idea to first get into neutral territory. For some people, it's simply too big a jump to affirm happiness or confidence when they are experiencing strong negative thoughts. Instead of saying *I am happy*, say *I am working on becoming happier*. Even just *I am feeling fine today*. Get to zero first. This can be a game changer.

DROP NEGATIVE WORDS

If you use words such as *don't* or *won't* in your affirmations, there is a chance that you will be attracting negative things back into your life. Instead, rephrase your affirmations. *I won't be eating junk food today* will change *to today, I will nourish myself with high-quality food*.

RELEASE

A simple yet effective affirmation is *I release*. This is helpful if you're feeling stressed or struggle with past events. Try to affirm *I release* when you feel you need it. This simple trick has helped many people I know.

TYPE EM' UP

I sometimes type up my affirmations and print them as this helps give everything a more formal and official note. Of course, if your affirmations include how you will take your boss' job in four months, then don't use the work printer - that could be awkward. Seeing your affirmations often, will help to forge new positive pathway in your brain. Stick them on the fridge.

AFFIRM HAPPINESS WHEN YOU NEED

I am truly happy or *It is normal for me to be happy*. Just as with *I release*, this simple affirmation can snap you out of overthinking in an instant, leading you to happier thoughts and a feeling of calm.

SMILE

You can fake your smile to achieve a happier reality, so in a way smiling is related to affirmations. Try practising to smile as often as possible during your day. It doesn't matter if putting on your smile feels forced or unnatural, because it's still effective in making you happier. When you smile, your body releases endorphins, dopamine and serotonin. These are neurotransmitters sometimes called your *happy chemicals*. When you smile, your thoughts and the way you feel automatically become more positive.

Once you become happier, you'll realise that your true smile is expressed through your eyes. This is often called your *inner smile*. Seeing someone with a beautiful inner smile instantly draws you to this person. You'll become this kind of person once you've developed your Happiness Button!

MAKE AFFIRMATIONS SENSORY

Visualise and make your affirmations as sensory as possible. Smells, feelings, touch, sounds, tastes. Dive into the world of the senses. Let your imagination help you affirm in the most powerful way.

TRY AFF-NORMATIONS

Although they have not received as much press as regular affirmations, it doesn't mean they aren't effective. As our friend Gavin Stephenson tells us, sometimes acting *as if* doesn't cut it. Try acting *as if it's <u>normal</u>*.

COMBINE WITH GRATITUDE

When I was younger, it was always easier to eat a vegetable I didn't like if I also had something yummy on my plate too. The same goes when we mix affirmations with gratitude. Affirmations can be hard to get used to, but it's fairly easy to find things to be grateful for in your life. If you combine your affirmations with gratitude, then you're more likely to stick to your affirmations. Gratitude exercises are the fish fingers to my peas and mashed potato. How you do it is up to you but try combining the two!

IN A NUTSHELL

- Affirmations are positive statements you repeat to yourself to challenge negative thoughts and self-sabotage.
- Affirmations can influence your conscious and unconscious mind and turn you into a positive and powerful human being!
- *Fake it till you make it* or *act as if* often work to deliver desired results
- Science and real-life experiences support the benefits of affirmations.
- What can you affirm? Anything as long as it's somewhat believable!
- Affirmations are not just for successful money-hungry millionaires. They also help to boost your happiness.
- Aff-normations can make affirmations more believable!
- The law of attraction works but you need to be clear what you desire and take ACTION to see results.
- Visualise, be exact, be realistic. Try different techniques and see what works for you.
- Repeat affirmations morning and night. Your mind will internalise them and start working towards attaining them.

SUMMARY OF STEPS

1. What Areas of Your Life Could Benefit from Affirmations?
2. What Affirmations Work for You?
3. Repeat Your Affirmations Daily
4. Get to Zero First
5. Drop Negative Words
6. Release
7. Type Em' Up
8. Affirm Happiness When You Need

9. SMILE

10. Make Affirmations Sensory

11. Try Aff-normations

12. Combine with Gratitude

ADDITIONAL RESOURCES

What other books can I read?

First and foremost, Louise Hay. We started this chapter with a quote from her. She's the founder of Hay House Publishing, one of the most successful publishing houses for self-help and inspirational books. Louise also happens to be one of the greatest writers to ever write about affirmations. She's viewed as one of the founders of *self-help* and has even jokingly been called "the closest thing to a living saint." Her book *I Can Do It Affirmations: How to Use Affirmations to Change Your Life* is great for anyone who wants to dive deeper into the topic of affirmations. Alternatively, the book *Gmorning, Gnight!: Little Pep Talks for Me & You* by Lin-Manuel Miranda, the creator of the Broadway show *Hamilton*, is light-hearted and beautifully written. There are also some beautiful illustrations in the book!

CHAPTER 7: COMPASSION

"Human nature is good, just as water seeks low ground. There is no man who is not good, just as there is no water that does not flow downward."

Mencius (Chinese Philosopher)

"Human nature is evil, and goodness is caused by intentional activity."

Xunzi (Chinese Philosopher)

The question over whether human beings are fundamentally good or evil has always been heavily debated. Are we good by nature and society corrupts us, or are we evil by nature and society manages to restore order? Is goodness part of human nature or an intentional choice? What even is *goodness*?

While I'm not going to attempt to answer this deeply philosophical question, let me share some insights from my life that might help shed some light on the issue. I used to think that the world and people around me were exclusively evil at heart. I believed that deep down, people are only driven by animalistic instincts. I thought I was probably evil myself. There's so much greed around us. People often act so selfishly and commit such horrible acts that you can't blame anyone for assuming that humans have an evil core. I remember having a long conversation with a housemate at university where I detailed how human beings are ultimately just there to backstab each other for their own gain. Pretty bleak. My worldview was dark and pessimistic or as I called it, realistic.

Learning about compassion and meeting incredibly kind-hearted people opened my eyes to realise a more promising side to us. Just as we can be evil, we also have the capacity to spread kindness and love. Karen Armstrong, author of the book *Twelve Steps to a Compassionate Life*, tells us that we are hardwired to be compassionate. The issue is that primitive instincts of selfishness and survival often override compassion. She argues that if we work on surpassing the limitations of our primitive instincts every day, we will make the world and our lives much happier. Lord Voldemort and your horrible co-worker might make you question how true this statement is but deep down, do people want to be evil?

When you were a kid, did you want to be a superhero/ princess or did you dream of being an evil villain? For most of you, the answer will have been the superhero or princess. Even infants often demonstrate behaviour that is intended to help others such as offering you their half-finished mashed up sandwich or saliva dripping dummy. Deep down, most of us want to spread love, kindness, and positivity. The desire for doing good just happens to get clouded by the stresses and pains of life.

To get back in touch with our desire to do good, we need to remove layers of negativity caused by bad experiences. Experiencing hurt, pain, isolation or hateful propaganda all happens to people as they go through life. When people are negative, it's not their fault and rarely their choice, but rather a reaction to the pain and unhappiness they have experienced in their own life. It's a genetic component or a survival-based instinct. The way you were raised is key here, given that much of our unconscious database and so-called traumas are first constructed in childhood (parents and future parents, take note).

We Have Work to Do: Negativity is Everywhere!

Negativity really is widespread in our societies. Let's take internet trolls as an example. You can go on any video-hosting platform right now and look for a popular video of a cute animal of your choice (piglets are usually my go-to). I can guarantee you that the video will have a fair few dislikes and negative comments. *How on earth can you comment 'terrible video' on a video of a cute piglet? Why would someone take time out of their day to leave such a remark about an innocent little being? Maybe the sound on the video is bad? Nope, the sound is crisp. Maybe the piglet is doing something rude? Nope, it's being cute as always.* The reason for the dislikes must be something else. When people feel negative inside, they often resort to spreading negativity outwards as a coping mechanism. Imagine a glass of water that is too full. Eventually, some water flows over the rim. It's the same with negativity and hurt. When people have too much of it, it starts spilling over into the lives of others.

"Hurt people, hurt people."

Will Bowen

If we move on from cute animal videos to those of any celebrity or public figure, you'll find even more wild internet trolls unloading their negativity and hurt onto the screen. Negativity is everywhere it seems. Of course, this chapter is not about internet trolls. This chapter is not about the online world at all. It's very hands-on and has a real social component to it. It's about deep human connection. To practise compassion in the best possible way, it's important to first understand the underlying processes of negativity. Now that we have cleared the air, it's time to dive deeper into compassion.

What Exactly is Compassion?

The word compassion originates from Latin, meaning 'co-suffering'. It means sharing and sympathising with another's suffering. Compassion is what empathy is built on. However, unlike many people assume, compassion and empathy are not the same. Empathy is feeling another person's pain and emotion as if it was your own. There's a focus here on the cognitive. When you are empathetic, you are putting yourself in the shoes of someone else so to speak (no, shoe size doesn't matter here). Compassion, on the other hand, is feeling love and kindness for a person in a difficult situation, no matter how big or small the problem. Going beyond the cognitive elements of just feeling empathetic, you act to express your compassion. You are here to listen, to offer understanding, to lend a helping hand. You are here to help them reduce their pain by showing them love and kindness through your actions. You want to see this person free from suffering. You're being compassionate.

Self-compassion

Importantly, compassion is not just about being kind to others. To be happy, we must also be kind to ourselves. It often goes unnoticed how unkind we can be to ourselves. It seems less harmful to call yourself an idiot or beat yourself up for doing something wrong than it would be to do this to someone else. This is because you are not always getting an immediate response or verbal negative reaction from yourself. To you, your thoughts really seem rational in that moment.

However, there's also a negative response when you are unkind to yourself. You become unhappier. Acceptance and compassion go hand in hand. Accept that it's okay you messed up. We are all trying to improve and it's a hard journey. You're human, we all make mistakes. Be kind to yourself. Practise self-love. Forgive yourself and treat yourself to some rest, a meal and peace of mind. That's self-compassion. The goal is to become a compassionate friend to yourself.

I released an EP recently with five songs called *Banana Peel EP*. Why *Banana Peel* you ask? Because I want to remind people that we all slip up from time to time but we're human, so there's no need to be so hard on ourselves. That's self-compassion.

Compassion is Key for Happiness

Compassion is an essential part of your Happiness Button. You need to take this information seriously and not just skim read this chapter while you watch your favourite show on Netflix (I know you better than you think). Practising compassion is much more than learning how to deal with the negativity around you, it's about building heartfelt human connections, sympathising with the suffering of others and yourself, and doing good deeds to spread love in the world. When you practise compassion every day, it will become a great source of happiness for you and others around you.

The Dalai Lama believes that happiness is based on compassion. Happiness based on compassion is sustainable and not fleeting such as buying new 'cool' things. I recently bought a new phone to improve the videos I post on social media. Can you believe that I didn't turn it on for a whole week? It was just sitting in my room in a box, unopened. This was an interesting observation to me because only a few years ago, I would have stayed up all night playing with the phone and feeling so happy. Now, my focus is on creating content that helps people, building deep human connections and being as compassionate as I can be.

The Benefits of Compassion

Compassion is powerful stuff that can change your life. It has helped to develop a feeling of warmth inside that radiates out into the lives of others. Developing more compassion in your life is always a win-win situation. You help others feel happier and in the process, you become happier yourself. *Are there any other benefits that come from being compassionate?* Yes! Compassion is taught in the US military and they don't joke around!

- ## Overcoming Difficulty

It's not only me.

It's easy to get caught in a victim mindset where you feel you're the only one suffering. By listening to and engaging with the suffering and pain of others, you realise that you are not the only one who suffers. You get away from thinking *why is it always me*, and your problems are put into the perspective of wider suffering which almost always makes your problems feel less severe. You see that suffering is part of life and your problems are the challenges you need to face. You've not been singled out to experience suffering, this is simply your share.

Everybody has suffering in their life. Living with and taking care of your own suffering is your responsibility, just like it is your responsibility to take out the bins or wash the plates once in a while (did you know that Jeff Bezos and Bill Gates, two of the richest men in the world, wash the dishes almost every night?). You are certainly not the only person in the world taking out bins or washing plates.

Become a Boss at Coping with Difficult Situations

Compassion makes you determined to cope and deal with your problems in the best possible way. You no longer run away from problems. Since you have practised listening to the suffering of others, problems no longer scare you as much. You no longer feel the need to run from everything but instead, you directly look difficulty in the eye. By helping others, you train yourself to help yourself. Furthermore, since you are also practising self-compassion, you don't beat yourself up constantly. This results in you overcoming difficulty much easier and not getting caught in a constant monologue of negativity. You tell the negative self-talk to shush and stop distracting you from being a boss at life.

- ## Bettering Yourself and Becoming More Successful

Become a Better Person by Listening to Others

When practising compassion, you start to care more about what others have to say. No, this doesn't mean you put more importance on the opinions of others than your own. Instead, you start to listen to what people are saying and start to engage with the stories they tell you. Many of us are very self-absorbed and pay only limited attention to what others are telling us about their lives unless it seems to overlap with our interests. That being said, every person carries some very valuable information within them that can change your life or viewpoint on something. All you must do is listen. Of course, not all of the information is interesting and useful, but try this exercise.

A Happiness Button Exercise

Tomorrow, try to pay attention to the words of others. Be interested in what people around you are saying (you can fake the being interested part if you have to). You will find that despite a few exceptions, something is interesting if you pay close attention. As you repeat this exercise, learn to filter out the irrelevant stuff and engage with the things you feel might be valuable. Often, you have to listen to a person anyway, so you might as well listen instead of wishing they'd stop talking.

It's rare to find people who genuinely listen to what you are saying. If people can sense that you are listening to them, they will undoubtedly develop a liking for you. When people like you more, they will want to help you more. In fact, listening skills are highly valued by employers as these are key to mastering communication. Of course, you should care about what people are saying and not just listen until that promotion hits your inbox folder. People can always sense if you are genuine. **Genuinely care as much as possible**.

Furthermore, people who are experiencing depression and anxiety tend to be quite absorbed in their own problems. Compassion can help during low points by allowing people to see beyond themselves and focus on doing good in other people's lives. Start listening to other people's stories and worries. Be interested. Be genuine. Be compassionate.

From Hurting Others to Wishing Them Well

When you re-train your mind to focus on feeling love and kindness for others, your whole perspective on life changes. When you start to be compassionate with people, it will become challenging to hurt others, even if they've done *you* wrong in the past. Being compassionate doesn't mean accepting the bad that people do to you or being passive about it. It's about looking beyond the superficial and childish layer of *you did this to me, so I will do this to you.*

You should have healthy boundaries and know when something has gone too far, and you should be able to react appropriately to solve the situation. It's perfectly fine to tell someone to be quiet if your intention is not to harm them. People will try to pull you into their swirl of negativity, but you should not let yourself be consumed by hate and negativity. You will never win in this game of getting others back for what they have done to you. You will never become happier by doing something terrible to someone. All this does is intensify the situation, spread more negativity, and damage your peace of mind.

• Build a Strong Support Network

I used to always bottle up my problems in the past but I have increasingly discovered the value in having a support network around me. There is so much weight lifted off your shoulders if you have someone you can talk to. When I was a student support worker at university, I first approached the role with the mindset *of I'm going to be a counsellor for these students and help them solve their problems with all this life experience and emotional intelligence I have.* I soon realised that the most helpful sessions were those where I merely sat back and attentively listened to the student - that was true support.

Being compassionate in life will really help you build up the support network you need to thrive. In essence, you are building up a support network of compassionate people who will be there for you since you helped them when they needed it. You showed them what compassion is, and they are now happy to try being compassionate with you too. If you're not giving people anything, why should they spend so much time listening to you?

Imagine you had a food stall in the city selling your favourite food. Two people approach your truck to ask for free food. One of them is a mechanic who once serviced your car for free when you had no money. The other person is someone you met through a friend but has never done anything for you apart from greeting you occasionally. Who are you more likely to give free food to? Probably the mechanic. Be there for people, and they will be there for you.

Let's not be naïve. Not everyone you meet with compassion will return the favour, and that's fine. The fact remains that the more you help others, the more others will help you. It's a numbers game. Building your network of supporters will help you activate your Happiness Button much quicker. Don't approach this as a business interaction, always be genuine and remember that we're all human beings that want to be accepted and loved. We all go through struggles.

I've compiled a list of some of the benefits you can expect when you practise being compassionate.

- Less stress
- More confidence
- More focus and clarity
- Better physical and mental health
- Closer and more social relationships
- A calmer mind (less anxious & insecure)
- An ability to overcome difficult situations easier
- A strong support network
- Less self-absorbed
- Developing your listening skills
- Good 'karma' (do good to others and others will do good to you)
- More attractive (we all love a kind person)
- Increased sense of life purpose
- Increased happiness

Real Life Examples of Applying Compassion

The volunteer-driven initiative *Karma Kitchen* serves FREE restaurant meals for people in over 20 cities worldwide. The menu and bill always read 0.00.

"Your meal was a gift from someone who came before you. To keep the chain of gifts alive, we invite you to pay it forward for those who dine after you".

You never pay for your own meal, but you pay for someone else's meal. No one <u>has</u> to pay as the price is zero, so if everyone decided not to pay, Karma Kitchen would be paying the meals for everyone and running at a huge loss. It's because of the good in people that the chain is kept alive. That's why Karma Kitchen works. A true community spirit and sense of doing something good for someone and others doing good for you can be felt with this initiative.

There's another incredible example of compassion at work. Based in India, eye hospital chain, *Aravind,* do 60% as many eye surgeries as the NHS in the UK and are vastly more cost-efficient. What's their secret and how does this relate to compassion? You might not believe it, but almost a third of their treatments are free! Poor people and those from rural villages are offered free treatment, travel and accommodation to tackle unnecessary blindness. Paying customers subsidise the free surgeries. Even the paying customers pay much less than at other hospitals, as the system runs ultra effectively (taking inspiration from the McDonald models of efficiency). This model of free treatments might seem unimaginable in some private health care systems around the world but it's also highly profitable and carries a real sense of compassion with it.

And lastly, a famous example to draw on is an experiment by Michael Norten and Elizabeth Dunn, professors at the Harvard Business School, which demonstrates the power of giving to others. Half of the study participants spent money on others, and half spent money on themselves. Those who spent money on others felt substantially happier than those who spoilt themselves. I've experienced this time, and time again in my own life. Helping others makes me feel good!

My mother sometimes tells me the story of how when I was in nursery, we were assigned the task of spending a small amount of money on whatever we liked. She said I spent half of the money on a fresh croissant and the other half I gave to a homeless man. I must have understood the power of giving and compassion at a young age!

Compassion is powerful and should have a key place in our life. Find those who need help and see how you can help them. This doesn't need to cost you anything. Sometimes, a listening ear is most powerful. People will not always ask for help, but if you approach them with compassion, they will sense it and often open up to you.

Steps to Happiness via Compassion

DO ACTS OF KINDNESS DAILY

This could be a small thing such as letting someone go in front of you in the supermarket queue or holding the door open for someone. It could be buying coffee for someone or even giving a small gift to a friend. It's a muscle you train and with time, you'll find it happens naturally.

When you carry out your acts of kindness, pay close attention to how you feel after you've done them. Do you feel happier and less stressed?

BE A LISTENING EAR

Instead of ignoring someone's attempt to share something with you, just listen and show compassion.

Truly listen and show others that you care about what they are saying. Do not get tempted to turn it into a counselling session (as I used to do) as then, the focus is on you trying to find a solution and boosting your ego. You can always make small suggestions here and there but focus on listening for now. If you do need to be somewhere or the situation has become uncomfortable, excuse yourself politely. Only give what you are capable of giving, no one can expect more from you. I used to let people talk on and on even if I felt uncomfortable or I had to be somewhere. I've learned to step out when I need to. It benefits everyone when we take good care of ourselves. We must be compassionate but also self-compassionate.

To truly feel compassionate and to understand a situation better, ask yourself, *Why is it that this person is experiencing pain and suffering? What is the real cause of their suffering?*

When it comes to suffering, people often code their pain as a self-defence mechanism. Many of us have a fear of being seen as weak. Try to establish the deeper source of suffering and show compassion. To help the other person, it's useful to find the source of suffering. When you identify it, you shouldn't keep bringing it up and poking at it. Your focus should be on listening and showing them that you're there to support them. Both of you will feel less alone and safer in this world. These types of connections are crucially important in an increasingly disconnected world.

My tip is to be very mindful of the situation. If it's appropriate, try to lighten the mood and show the person that not all is bad. This isn't essential but it can be helpful in certain situations. I am a joker myself. I always try to lighten the mood or bring a sense of optimism when possible. Most importantly, compassion is about showing that you care.

TRY THE 'WE'RE NOT SO DIFFERENT' EXERCISE

When you encounter someone (perhaps even a pet), remind yourself that when it comes down to it, you are not so different. Everyone needs to eat and a place to sleep. Everyone wants to be successful, everyone wants to be happy and everyone wants to be loved. There are many differences between us but there are also a lot of things we have in common.

Whenever you meet someone, think to yourself: *This person wants to be successful, just like I do, this person wants to be happy, just like I do, this person wants a slice of pizza, just like I do* …and so on!

It becomes easier to offer compassion when you become aware of the things you have in common with a person. Other people have many of the same needs and struggles that you do. In fact, you won't find anyone in the world who does not share a few core commonalities. To dive into the more spiritual side of compassion, we could also argue that *all is one* and there are no differences between us on a deeper level. We're all made up of particles, we all bleed red, we're all consciousness, and we all die one day. From this perspective, our differences are rather superficial.

VOLUNTEER

"Remember that the happiest people are not those getting more, but those giving more."

H. Jackson Brown Jr. (American author)

Volunteering for a good cause is not only a great way to give back to your community, but also a good way to practise compassion and in turn, increase your happiness. You are acting compassionately to the fact that others need help and assistance in their life. You are there to give them your time as a gift and help to make their life easier. You are doing good for others who need help which will also make you feel great about yourself.

Service to others is the rent you pay for your room here on Earth

Muhammad Ali

There are some fantastic volunteering opportunities near you, just Google it. Akin to listening skills, volunteering also looks great on any CV. You don't need to join an organisation to start volunteering. There are always people in your family or community who will benefit from your help. Could you help your grandmother in the garden? Could you help your cousin with some cooking to take some stress off their shoulders? Don't forget Mother Earth either - she always benefits from people keeping her healthy.

VISIT WORKSHOPS, EVENTS, RESTAURANTS THAT 'PAY IT FORWARD'.

Karma kitchen is a perfect example of *a pay it forward* initiative. If you buy a coffee for a stranger, you're probably one of the only people doing it that day. The person you're buying it for might not accept your generosity because it's so unusual. They might even be suspicious of your motive but that shouldn't stop you from paying it forward.

Check out the Museum of Happiness in the UK for workshops and events. Feel free to share any information about such organisations in the *MyHappinessButton* Facebook group. Let's start creating a directory of movement from around the world!

GIVE TO CHARITY

"No one has ever become poor by giving."

Anne Frank

There are always natural disasters, inequalities or tragedies around the world that urgently need support. Do your best to give what you can. It will strengthen your sense of compassion and help others immensely. Giving will make you feel more abundant as you focus less on not having enough. You could even start your own campaign to motivate friends and members of the public to donate to a cause of your choice. See websites such as gofundme.com or justgiving.com

Realise how fortunate you are. Don't give with the intention to feel good about yourself. Give with the intention to help. Be of service. With this mindset, you'll naturally feel good.

DON'T HATE THE HATEFUL

This step is about being kind and loving to those who are hateful. Again, this is not about being passive but instead, it's about not letting yourself be consumed by negativity. It isn't about rejecting your feelings either. If you do feel hateful towards another person, then shine the light of awareness on it. This step is about aiming to understand why this hateful person is feeling so hateful. Were they born this way? What happened to them to make them like this? What happened over the last year, or this morning, or in the last 10 minutes? You are not doing yourself a favour by hating the hateful. Their hate will become yours. Darkness can't drive out darkness, only light can do that.

I often have discussions with a friend of mine about this topic. He believes that you need to respond with hate to show the other person that they can't mess with you. He thinks that if you are too kind to hateful people, they will keep using you as a dumpster for their hate. He makes a fair point. The haters will certainly be back if they realise you're an easy target. However, you have a trick up your sleeve.

Compassion!

React with love and kindness and don't let the hate consume you. Keep reminding yourself that there is a reason why this person is suffering. The hate is not about you but about them feeling bad! It's *their* full glass flowing over into *your* life. If it's hard for you to act with compassion in the moment, remove yourself from the situation and take some deep breaths. Reflect on the situation. *Why is this person suffering?* Bring them to mind and wish them well. With practise, hate will massively decrease in your life and you will feel a lot happier and less tense.

From my own experience, I don't think my friend is right. When you respond with kindness instead of hate, many hateful people will leave you alone. Their goal is to make you feel hateful too. If you don't accept it, they'll stop trying to unload it onto you. If they can sense even a spark of hate in you, they'll probably keep trying.

These people are not evil monsters, they are injured beings. Their glass is too full. It can't help but overflow.

PRACTISE 'LOVING-KINDNESS' MEDITATION

So, here's the low down. With loving-kindness meditation, you first show yourself unconditional love and then extend it to all beings. It's about repeating certain phrases to yourself. *I am worthy of being loved, I am happy and healthy, I am kind to myself.*

You then extend this love to friends, family, strangers and finally, those you find troubling.

It's not about anyone *deserving* love and kindness but about recognising that all beings have the right to be loved unconditionally. Love is a feeling of peace and your purest essence. I know that sounds like an overused quote from a movie, but it's true if you think about it.

Try a loving-kindness meditation on *Insight Timer* or similar apps. Meditation classes also offer these kinds of guided meditations very often. Although loving-kindness meditation stems from Buddhism, you can practise it regardless of your religious orientation. Love and kindness are universal. The meditation works unconsciously but you will feel more love, empathy and compassion for people very soon. You might still get irritated by people, but they won't ruin your day anymore.

PRACTISE SELF-COMPASSION

Putting yourself down can have serious consequences. It can diminish your feeling of self-worth and even make you develop anxiety or depression. If you want to be happy, you should try to practise self-compassion.

So how do you practise self-compassion?

Self-compassion means seeing things crystal clear. You are not distorting reality. You are mindful to what is here right now. When you are feeling good, then you are feeling good. When you are feeling bad, then you are feeling bad. You become aware of exactly what you are experiencing, and you are kind to yourself regardless. Offer yourself love and kindness. Be a good supportive friend to yourself. With self-compassion, you accept everything as it is.

When you are compassionate with others, you see that you are not the only one suffering. This understanding is key for self-compassion. Remind yourself that suffering is okay. You are not the only one suffering. You are not being weak, you are being human. Loving-kindness meditation and affirmations will also develop your sense of self-compassion.

If you have been through trauma, it can be crucial to work with a therapist to get you to a stage of genuine self-compassion. Not only can a therapist get you there quicker than working by yourself, they can also help you deal with overwhelming feelings if they come up. Self-compassion feels amazing. You deserve it. It's time to become your own best friend.

IN A NUTSHELL

- Although we have the capacity to do bad, we equally have the capacity to be loving and kind.

- Hurt, pain, isolation, hateful propaganda, genetic components and primitive instincts influence our level of negativity and hate.

- We have work to do. Negativity is everywhere! (even on videos of cute piglets).

- People who suffer from negativity try to unload it onto others. Think of the full glass of negativity flowing over into the lives of others. Hurt people, hurt people.

- Good news, we are hardwired to be compassionate!

- Empathy and compassion are not the same. Empathy is acknowledging someone's pain mentally. Compassion is showing acts of love and kindness towards the person suffering.

- Compassion is not just a way to deal with the negative. It's crucial for building heartfelt human connections, sympathising with the suffering of others and doing good deeds to spread love in the world.

- Listening with the intention to offer understanding is key for compassion.

- By being compassionate, you go beyond the victim mentality. You find it easier to overcome difficulties. You become a better, more likeable, more knowledgeable and more successful person. You build strong support networks.

- Compassion can become a key source of happiness for you.

- The Dalai Lama believes happiness to be based mostly on compassion.

- To be happy, we also must practise self-compassion.

- There are many examples of organisations and initiatives that have demonstrated the value of compassion for happier people and better societies.

- A compassionate life is exciting, involves a deep connection with others and brings many benefits with it.

SUMMARY OF STEPS

1. Do Acts of Kindness Daily
2. Be a Listening Ear
3. Try the *'We Are Not So Different'* Exercise
4. Volunteer
5. Visit Workshops, Events, Restaurants that 'Pay it Forward'
6. Give to Charity

7. Don't Hate the Hateful
8. Practise 'Loving-Kindness' Meditation
9. Practise Self-compassion

ADDITIONAL RESOURCES

Want to know more about **Karma Kitchen**? Visit: http://www.karmakitchen.org/

Further Reading? If you would like to read some more on how to develop compassion and self-compassion, I recommend the book *Self Compassion: The Proven Power of Being Kind to Yourself* by Dr.Kristin Neff - she's a top dog when it comes to the topic.

CHAPTER 8: ENJOY THE JOURNEY & EMBRACE CHANGE

Frankie Cote, a good friend of mine from the UK has truly experienced the highs and lows that life has to offer. At age 21, he performed songs he wrote as a teenager in his bedroom to crowds of up to 1,400 people. He's even been a radio presenter and a director of Strategic Partnerships at a tech-firm in Canada. I will also add that he is extremely funny, talented and likeable, so none of the above should surprise you in the slightest.

At the same time, he is a recovering alcoholic, former drug user and has had two failed suicide attempts. He's seen the lows of life, to say the least.

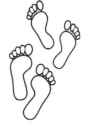

Today, Frankie is travelling the world, living out his purpose and teaching people how to transform their lives. What his story shows us is that no matter how low or high life gets, the past or future do not matter. You can always find your bliss in the present moment if you truly embrace life and accept that life has highs and lows as part of the journey.

Life's Not a Journey but a Dance

Another reason why I am bringing up Frankie is because he opened my eyes to the idea that it might not be helpful to call life a journey. In a video titled *Life is NOT a journey*, he gets real philosophical on us (I'm okay with that). Frankie explains how people often use the concept of 'life is a journey' to facilitate an unsatisfactory life. People are justifying unhappiness and not going out of their comfort zone. They use *the journey* as an excuse for being miserable right now because after slaving away in an office cubicle for 20 years, they might have saved up enough money to travel the world and be happy. Many of us justify the undesirable things we're too scared to change as part of the journey. It's our excuse.

Frankie argues that life is only a journey in so far that we die at the end. The time between your birth and death you can call your journey. Otherwise, there's just the here and now. *This is it!* In the here and now, there is no journey, there is only existence. You can shape your existence how you like. There will be obstacles and struggles, but don't hold on to an illusionary idea of a journey to justify being stuck in your ways.

Instead, we should look at life as a dance or piece of music. The legendary philosopher, Alan Watts famously said that you *play* the piano, you don't *work* it. The best conductors are not those who are first to finish a song. The best dancers are not those who finish the song first either. The best are those who present the most beautiful piece in the moment. The point is not the final destination but the process itself. This metaphor directly applies to life! Many of us are too focused on our final destination. As a result, we often forget to enjoy our life. We don't treat life like a dance but more like a race. We're always under pressure as we feel we're falling behind. You don't always need to achieve a result or reach a destination as the idea of a journey suggests. Every single moment is here and now and holds the potential for happiness and a fulfilled life.

The Destination is a Myth

We often think that at the finish line, we'll find wealth and happiness and all of our problems will be solved. We focus on the gold at the end of the rainbow and not the beauty of the rainbow itself. In this book, we have explored several times that external things will not bring us fulfilment. The destination will only provide a limited and fleeting feeling of joy. You'll get to your destination and then start looking for a new destination. That's how we work. You get the gold at the end of the rainbow and then start searching for a new pot of gold soon after.

What Alan Watts and my friend Frankie are telling us, is that the key to a fulfilled life is not to reach your destination but to make the destination less important. Instead, our focus should be on enjoying the process itself.

"Focus on the journey, not the destination. Joy is found not in finishing an activity but in doing it."

Greg Anderson

Even if you're not where you would like to be career-wise, enjoy everything about where you are right now. Enjoy the failures. See them as opportunities to grow and be present to those unforgettable moments happening around you all the time. There's so much to be grateful for. It's all about the dance.

I am going to keep repeating it until everybody is saying it in their sleep. *Enjoy the process of life rather than getting too fixed on an end goal.* Some people tend to get fixated on the destination, thinking they can only be happy when they have earned their right to be happy. Does that mean in all the time it takes to get to the destination you cannot be happy? What if you die before you reach the destination?

There will be successes and failures. That's the beauty of life. You learn to embrace the unpredictability of life and stay excited about what will come up. Enjoy the dance, journey, or whatever you want to call it.

Let your life flow and let things happen naturally. When you are fixated on the destination, then you often block your path which can lead to you not making the best decisions you could be making. I have seen this with my music. When I was constantly refreshing my statistics page to see if I had any more likes, comments or followers, my music was going nowhere. When I started enjoying the process and took a step back, I saw a change for the better.

Did I Get the Title of this Chapter Wrong?

Felix, you keep talking about this dance of life, yet you called this chapter Enjoy the Journey. Okay, I'll give it to you, this chapter could benefit from being called *Enjoy the Dance of Life & Embrace Change*, as that seems to be what I'm rambling on about. However, there's a good reason why I stuck with the word *journey*.

Mortality, which awaits us at the end of our journey, is a massive motivator to enjoy every single moment. That's why I chose to stick with it. This doesn't mean that you shouldn't think of life in terms of a dance to be enjoyed. Instead, better enjoy this beautiful dance, and be okay when you fall or don't make the perfect move. One day, when your journey comes to an end, you won't be able to dance any longer. Mortality motivates us to make the most of our days and live our happiest life. Part of the reason why I managed to write this book is that I reminded myself repeatedly that I don't know how long I have left to live, and I want to gift the world with my tips for a happier life.

Discover and Live Your Purpose

"He who has a why to live for can bear almost any how."
Friedrich Nietzsche

You can think of discovering your purpose as: *What is the dance that most fulfils me?* Discovering and living your purpose is what will make you jump out of bed in the morning. Eckhart Tolle told us that being present should be our primary life purpose, and that should fuel us already. Yet, we also have our secondary life purpose that can massively motivate us, create good in the world and contribute to our happiness. In the western world, it's difficult to only live out your primary purpose of being present. Your secondary life purpose, when well defined, will allow you to flourish in society.

What does your purpose have to do with happiness?

Many people require a sense of progress and purpose to feel happy. The authors of *Ikigai* (Garcia and Miralles) conducted a range of interviews with Okinawans, many of them being over 100 years old. The Okinawans live on a small island near the coast of mainland Japan and although it's one of the poorest places in Japan, its people are often regarded as an extremely happy bunch! Part of the reason they are so happy is their *Ikigai*. *Ikigai* loosely translates to 'a reason for being', or 'being happy with being busy'. Being happy with being busy may sound like the opposite of

There will be successes and failures. That's the beauty of life. You learn to embrace the unpredictability of life and stay excited about what will come up. Enjoy the dance, journey, or whatever you want to call it.

happiness to some of us. Yet, being busy isn't a problem if you enjoy the activity you're doing! Having an *Ikigai* means acting from a state of mind where people feel at ease. During the practise of *Ikigai*, people often experience a state of flow. You can compare this to the feeling you get when you get lost in doing something you really enjoy. For example, painting or making music (*insert your hobby here*).

The authors of *Ikigai* conclude that the happiest people are not those who get the most done in life but those who spend more time in a state of flow. When you are doing something you're passionate about, you will most likely find yourself in a state of flow. Imagine how amazing it would feel to experience moments of flow every single day? That's why it's important to discover your purpose and live it.

Another friend of mine, Tony Shavers III is the best-selling author of the book *Is Your Dream Really Worth It?* He helps you break down any limiting beliefs you might have that are holding you back from living out your dream life. Tony helps you set up a step-by-step plan to discover and live your purpose. You will stop thinking *Oh I can't be a salsa dancer* and will start saying *Where's the nearest salsa class*?! If you want to achieve anything, then you can find a way to do it once you've got your mind and goals aligned with this vision.

If you want to discover your purpose, ask yourself what hobby or work you would be doing if this was your last day on earth. There's a good chance the answer is closely related to your purpose and an activity that will induce this desirable state of flow. This is the *why* Nietzsche refers to in the quote above.

To discover your purpose, you can also do a future self-meditation. In this meditation, you'll discover what your heart desires. I usually find myself surrounded by nature and teaching workshops to increase happiness - it's a pretty insightful exercise. My future self is always really kind, funny and surprisingly muscular.

Anticipation and Contentment:
Why You Need It

It's hard to say who I like more, Eckhart Tolle or Prince Ea. Both of them inspired me and changed my life tremendously. Prince Ea is like the younger, cooler version of Eckhart. He reminds us of the importance of presence and creates engaging and fun-to-watch motivational videos. Prince Ea created a *YouTube* video called *THE COMMERCIAL THEY DON'T WANT YOU TO SEE*. In the video, he tells a teenage boy who has been waiting in line to get a new smartphone that it was not the phone that made him happy but the release from the craving of wanting the phone. He argues that the fix is not new things but contentment. It's nothing short of amazing and brings this point to life nicely.

Although anticipation can be linked with the frustration of not having enough, I do think anticipation has its place in a happy and balanced life. How nice will it be when your brother comes to visit for Christmas? How amazing will it feel to chill out on a beach in Cuba? Anticipation can generate a bunch of positive emotions and give us something to look forward to when life gets challenging. Some spiritual teachers will tell you that all that matters is the present moment, and that a future event should not occupy any of your mental space. Living in the present is important, but some feelings of anticipation are perfectly healthy in my opinion. As long as you don't assume that getting there holds the key to fulfilment.

I often find that the excitement before meeting up with friends is just as sweet as actually meeting up. The excitement before the holiday is just as lovely as being there. However, anticipation should only be used in controlled and small doses or else you will start to make your happiness and fulfilment dependent on these external things occurring.

Even more important than small doses of anticipation, are large doses of contentment. Get out of the habit of *wanting* and be content with what you have. This is largely done by practising gratitude. As Prince Ea said in his video, contentment is key when it comes to living a fulfilled life.

Avoid self-talk which tells you *I can't be happy until I have this*, or *I can't be happy until I am that*.

As young children, we are often in a state of contentment. Unless we had one of our crazy *wanting* sprees at the supermarket. In adult life, the desire of *wanting* is a root cause of our unhappiness. Be happy with the unique opportunity you were gifted with to walk this earth. It's about giving up those constant *wants* and enjoying your life as it is right now.

Embrace Change

Change is closely linked to uncertainty and strong emotions. Sayings such as *never change a winning team* or *if it ain't broke, don't fix it* suggest to us that change should be avoided at all costs. It's important to realise that change is a natural part of life and needs to be accepted, not resisted. If you resist change, then you will end up struggling. To start easing off this resistance, let's consider two examples.

If nothing ever changed, there would be no butterflies. If the caterpillar never changed, it would always remain a little worm without beautiful wings (not hating on caterpillars, they are beautiful in their own right, but they can't fly!).

Equally, imagine you're a surfer and life is an ocean filled with giant waves; you won't be able to ride one wave forever. The different waves represent change and a different opportunity. Maybe this new wave will be your best ride ever? It's crucially important to stay afloat and embrace the wave. If you try to resist the wave or wish back a previous one, you'll get knocked down hard. There's a risk of drowning (in real life).

The Importance of Adaptability

The happiest and most successful people are those who have mastered the skill of adaptability. A key component is accepting new circumstances and even finding opportunities within the change.

When I moved from Germany to the UK at seven years old, I hated the change. I would stay indoors all day for months. Looking back, I think it was a change for the better. As a result, I learned to speak English from a young age, which allowed me to connect with incredible people in my life who I might not have met otherwise. I probably also wouldn't be creating music in English and maybe not even writing this book. Because of the change, I have more opportunities than if I had stayed in the small German city I was born in.

When I started to get sick, this was a drastic change. I couldn't meet friends as I used to. I didn't have the same energy levels that I used to.

Would I ever feel the same again? I resisted the change, and I suffered as a result. If I had been open to all the blessings that resulted from the change, I could have gone without much of the suffering. We never know what might come, we just have to embrace change and be open to the blessings and opportunities it holds.

Some more benefits of change

- You grow stronger as a person
- You switch up your routine (creating a sense of excitement)
- You will be faced with new opportunities
- You re-consider your values (resulting in breakthroughs)

(Source: tinybuddha.com)

The dance of life would be boring if you only ever made the same move. The surfer doesn't always want to ride the same wave. Sometimes your moves will and should change. It's important not to become dependent on this illusionary concept of the past by not living in the present. Be present to change and experience life as it unfolds.

Change most likely involves going outside of your comfort zone – this calls for what is possibly my favourite quote of all time.

"Life begins at the end of your comfort zone."
Neale Donald Walsch

Nothing in Life is Permanent

It's very important to remind yourself of the fact that nothing in life is permanent. No relationships, no objects, not even yourself. Although a red light at a junction might make you question this fact, nothing lasts forever! It can sometimes be a hard pill to swallow. Our days on this planet are counted and it's up to us to make the most of them. When you can accept that and see that the opportunity of life is incredible regardless, then you can treat the simple fact of existing as a massive success and reason to celebrate. Enjoy being alive. Make it count.

"There is nothing permanent except change."
Heraclitus

"Life, if well lived, is long enough."
Seneca

Inner Peace ≠ Lacking Ambition

There's a myth that says when we find more inner peace, we start to become as complacent and lazy as a sloth. This doesn't have to be the case. When I first read *The Power of Now* by Eckhart Tolle, I went too far on the *being present* side of things and became almost careless about everything in my life. *Career? Who cares?!* With time, I discovered that it's perfectly fine and necessary to have a sense of ambition in life. Many of us need something to strive towards to stay sane. Ambition can fuel us!

Does this scenario sound familiar?

You get two weeks holiday from work. The first day you relax, throw on some Netflix, do whatever you like. After a while, you start to feel a tickling sensation that calls for your attention. Your mind wants to start doing productive things again. If you're not careful, you can find yourself immersed in work e-mails and back on the work grind, even though you're supposed to be on vacation!

We always need a challenge or task to make us feel that we're progressing. From a simple evolutionary standpoint, being complacent does not feel good. You gravitate towards work because there might not be any other productive outlet you have in your life. Find some projects that help build the best version of yourself and improve the world around you. You could volunteer or start building something. Whatever comes to mind and seems practical.

Just because you're developing inner peace and tuning into presence, this doesn't mean you should shy away from challenges. If you stop being ambitious, you're doing the world a disservice. If I stopped being ambitious, I would not have published this book. I would not have recorded 40+ songs. I would be missing out on all the great connections I will make due to my creations. Being ambitious is okay! You just have to ensure you keep your inner peace and ambition balanced.

If you need further guidance, please reach out to me. I've gone through the struggle of finding the balance and still do to this day. I certainly have some practical advice for you.

Stay Curious – It'll Make You Feel Alive

Staying curious is crucial to a fulfilled life. If you think you know all about your environment, take the opportunity to expose yourself to a new environment (or relationship) or pay closer attention to the one you're in. Notice new elements to it and be present. You could also travel to different countries or meet new people. While this can be exciting, you don't need to tire yourself out or blow the budget to stay curious. You also don't need to meet new people to hear new stories. You just need to be curious and ask the people you know different questions. When they feel your curiosity and compassion, they will open up.

Within a boring job, there are 1000's of things you could be doing differently to bring you enjoyment. When I was working in a sports shop, I was tasked with the job of selling an extra pair of socks with every pair of shoes. There was no additional commission. This could have been a boring task. However, I remained curious and tried to see how good my selling skills were. By the end of the day, I was the best salesman in the entire store and my boss even mentioned my selling skills in a team meeting. All because I remained curious while selling socks! Is there anything you could be doing differently at work? Could you improve the efficiency of your workplace? Could you find ways to uplift the mood?

If you want to be happy, never treat life as boring or assume that you know everything about your environment. If you stay curious and pay attention, you will be rewarded with much excitement.

If You're in a Rut, You Won't Always Be

Life is tough. Tell me about it. Just like my friend Frankie, I've seen severe lows in life. This book is the direct result of me overcoming a seriously low episode. It's important to remember that if you're feeling down or you're in a difficult place, these feelings will also pass. Whenever I've had depressive moods, I'm overcome by the feeling that I'll be stuck in this forever. This is irrational. Your life and your mood can completely change within a short time.

There are countless stories of people who were in the lowest of lows but managed to turn their life around quickly. Burnell Washburn is one of them, a very positive artist and friend of mine from Utah. We've worked on a song together and he sometimes rocks my clothing brand

Gratitude=Abundance in his videos. Life hasn't always been so positive for Burnell. A few years ago, he was in a real rut. He struggled financially and even got his car repossessed on his birthday. If you look at his videos, you'd struggle to find a more blissful or happy individual on *YouTube*. Life can change quickly for you too. This too will pass.

H.O.P.E = Hold On, Pain Ends.

Happiness is Not an End State

Despite me talking about enjoying the journey, there's no destination. There's never a point where you can say: *right, now I have reached ultimate happiness.* This might be frustrating to hear but the goal is just to dance beautifully, to learn some new steps and to enjoy your existence. You don't need to stress about accumulating more and more happiness. You just need to tune into your body and mind and do things that feel right for you. Build up your Happiness Button.

The point is to develop the skill of happiness throughout your life. Enjoy every moment as much as possible and live in the present. You won't finally be happy once you've achieved something. Things will never be perfect. It's about accepting the imperfect dance as if it were perfect. Just dance. Live life, it's beautiful. Being alive, being present, being accepting, being grateful, being compassionate and being in the process of developing a mindstate of happiness is already the destination. You have already achieved it.

"Happiness is the experience of climbing toward the peak."

Tal Ben-Shahar

Steps to Happiness via Enjoy the Journey & Embrace Change

STAY CURIOUS BY ASKING QUESTIONS

When you were a kid, you were terrific at asking questions. We become so occupied with ourselves during our adult life that when someone asks a meaningful question, we jump at the opportunity to answer. We have moved from asking to answering. Try to see if you can ask someone a meaningful question and listen carefully for those interesting bits of information. This will allow you to build deeper relationships.

When asking meaningful questions, don't restrict yourself to those close to you. Staying curious means asking questions when you feel like it. Ask the bus driver where he got those sleek new glasses. Try to keep curiosity alive at all times. Curiosity can also just mean being present and observant. You don't always need to spark up a conversation, curiosity can happen in silence. Just sit back and curiously observe (without being creepy of course).

Learn something new about people and the world around you every single day. Whatever it is, this world is an endlessly exciting place if you are ready to listen, observe and ask.

TRY, TRY, TRY AND TRACK

It can be a good idea to try a range of different things and track how you felt when doing them. You will identify what most fulfils you in this dance of life. It's key to try different things and step out of your routine. Keep track of when you feel good after an activity. Write down what it was and with whom you did it. After some time, look back at what has accumulated on your list and do more of those activities going forward.

STAY IN MOTION TOWARDS YOUR PURPOSE

To feel that you're moving closer to living the meaningful life you desire, it's essential that you take action related to your purpose. If your dream life is to be an artist then get creative every day, even if it's just a couple of sketches on a napkin. Attend exhibitions, go to networking events. Simply be in motion. Either practise your craft or take action to take you closer to living the life you desire. Baby steps are totally fine. You just need some sense of progress and motion towards your dreams.

EMBRACE YOUR MORTALITY

Let your understanding of mortality be your secret weapon to making the most of this life. People often ask me how I manage to juggle all I do and still create high-quality content... I create every piece of work as if it could be my last. With this mindset, I am more present, more driven and more active in enjoying life.

Outshine all of your competition and become the best version of yourself. Don't waste your precious time on this planet. Soak in the sun rays like there's no tomorrow. Taste every flavour in your meal. Mortality shouldn't depress you, but since there is no escaping from it, it's your reminder to truly enjoy this unique and marvellous opportunity you were given on earth. Enjoy the journey.

SPEND MORE TIME IN NATURE

This may be the most commonly given advice next to *drink more water*. It's so simple yet effective. Connecting with nature helps in almost every situation. In my humble opinion, the dance of life is best enjoyed in Mother Nature.

"Nature holds the key to our aesthetic, intellectual, cognitive and even spiritual satisfaction."

E.O. Wilson (Biologist)

TRAVEL

The diversity of landscapes and cultures is nothing short of mind-blowing. My first trip to Japan proved this to me. Start to explore different places. Whether it's far or near to home, it all counts. Travelling gives you a sense of freedom and new perspectives. It gives you a sense that there is more to life than your routine. It gives you a sense of being alive, and a strong sense of curiosity.

CHANGE IS NEVER YOUR ENEMY. IT'S JUST PART OF LIFE

If you can recognise that change is naturally part of life and should not be resisted then you will flow through life with ease. Don't let fear get in the way. Try to spot the opportunities for growth.

STOP LOOKING AT OTHER PEOPLE'S GRASS

Don't live by the mindset that *the grass is always greener on the other side*. Look at your own grass and maintain it well. Water it with proper nutrients. *Their* grass looks great, but so does yours and you don't see all the hard work or pesticides they are putting into it. Without getting too lost in this metaphor, ditch the comparing mindset. Just because someone else does well, does not make your dance any less amazing. Comparison will rob you of your peace and happiness. Look after your own garden. Let that grass flourish and sprout.

HAVE THINGS TO LOOK FORWARD TO

A small dose of anticipation can be healthy and boost your happiness. This could mean arranging meetings with friends, attending a workshop or planning a small trip. Put it in the diary. Then, be present to the feelings of anticipation. Enjoy it and let it carry you through more difficult times. Don't overuse anticipation to bring you happiness. Handle with care!

UPHOLD YOUR RESPONSIBILITIES

Professor Jordan Peterson, the rockstar academic from Canada, describes responsibility as the core of a meaningful life. Responsibility will justify the sacrifices you make and help you keep going, even when things get tough. It's almost like your north star of life, keeping you on track. Figure out your responsibilities and live by them; accept them as useful. Your responsibility to sweep the floor five times after work is unlikely to fulfil you. Your responsibility to take your kids to school is more likely to give you a sense of meaning. Adhering to responsibilities you accept as useful will most likely make you a better human being. There's much happiness to be found in responsibility and doing good.

GET OUT OF THE HABIT OF WANTING

"If you desire many things, many things will seem few."
Benjamin Franklin

It's important that you're not always in a mindset of *scarcity* and *wanting*. Although finding and pursuing a purpose is desirable, it doesn't override contentment, expressing gratitude, practicing acceptance or being present to life.

IN A NUTSHELL

- As my friend Frankie says, don't use *life's a journey* to justify an unsatisfactory life.

- There's value in looking at life as a dance. The goal is to make the process beautiful and not reach an end-point quickly.

- Give yourself the right to be happy now. Don't wait for a final destination. There's no end goal of happiness, it's something we develop and work on throughout our life.

- Find your purpose (*Ikigai*) and live it. It will make your life more meaningful. A sense of responsibility is a great guiding principle for life and justifies the sacrifices you make.

- Stay curious about everything in your life. There's so much to explore that you didn't know. Curiosity will make you feel alive.

- Your life should hold some anticipation but *A LOT* of contentment.

- Change should never be resisted. Instead, you should develop the skill of adaptability. Ride the waves of change like a surfer!

- Mortality is an inventible change. Use it to fuel your life.

- When developing inner peace, your ambitions and sense of progress do not fly out the window. You can be at peace while remaining ambitious to change your life and the world for the better.

- Get out of the habit of *wanting*. Gratitude and contentment are key.

- If you're feeling down - don't worry, this feeling will pass. You won't always feel the same. Your life can change quickly! I'm living proof of it.

SUMMARY OF STEPS

1. Stay Curious by Asking Questions

2. Try, Try, Try and Track

3. Stay in Motion Towards Your Purpose

4. Embrace Your Mortality

5. Spend More Time in Nature

6. Travel

7. Change is Never Your Enemy. It's Just Part of Life

8. Stop Looking at Other People's Grass

9. Have Things to Look Forward to

10. Uphold Your Responsibilities

11. Get Out of the Habit of *Wanting*

ADDITIONAL RESOURCES

Adaptability: In his *book Adaptability: How to Survive the Change You Didn't Ask*, behavioural strategist, Dr.Max McKeown draws on historical events to demonstrate how adaptability is vital for survival and happiness. By the way, how cool is the job of a behavioural strategist?! They study the conscious and unconscious biases of decision making within organisations.

How to escape any rut? Check out the book *ESCAPE, BREATHE, IGNITE!: How To Escape Any Rut* by my friend Frankie Cote.

CHAPTER 9: FACE YOUR FEARS & NEGATIVE EMOTIONS

Before we get started on this chapter, let's draw attention to two key points:

- What we think, how we feel, and the emotions we experience is never the problem. The problem is how we respond!

- There's no such a thing as *negative*. Good and bad are mental constructs. Shakespeare's Hamlet says, "for there is nothing either good or bad but thinking makes it so". Often, we respond according to how society labels emotions and thoughts. Emotions are just energy in motion. There's energy flowing through us, and it's up to us how we respond to it. I will still use the words negative and positive as they are useful for explaining the issue but be aware that they're just mental constructs.

When my grandfather passed away last year, it was very shocking news. He was such a big inspiration in my life. In his final years, he lived with illness to the point where he was unable to walk or care for himself. He didn't have it easy in life, but he always told my siblings and me that whatever life throws at you, you have to keep on going to succeed. No matter how slim the chance may be, you must keep going. You will succeed one day. He was incredibly inspiring.

Before attending his funeral, I felt many strong emotions surface. Sadness that he was no longer with us, and regret that I never spent enough time with him. I paid full attention to the sadness in me. I accepted it, I was aware of it; I was in the present moment with it. When I went to the funeral, I was okay. I didn't label the feeling as negative, I faced all my emotions in the present moment. Of course, I was sad. Of course, I shed a tear.

Dealing with Pain

The avoidance of pain only increases it. To heal, I had to pass through the doorway of grief. Emotional wounds are beyond sadness, they're felt in the depths of your being. Honour your pain and don't run from it. If you need, unplug from the world, put time aside to reflect and give yourself permission to grieve. That's how I coached myself and it worked. If well-meaning people push you to *get over it,* then ignore them and take however long you need to deal with pain. Surround yourself with friends who understand that.

Things I learnt as a result of this understanding

- My sadness didn't grow more than it needed because I faced it and didn't label it as *negative.* Avoiding pain only increases it.
- It was easier for me to get over my grandad's death because I was fully accepting of rising emotions and didn't resist them.
- It strengthened my sense of presence. I would return to the present moment to *feel* rather than getting lost in my mind to *think.*
- I was able to heal myself.

As author Holly Ruttenbur Dickinson puts it, "*face it, feel it, then heal it.*"

The Value of Facing Your Emotions

My Happiness Button is not about always feeling happy and on top of the world. Life naturally brings ups and downs with it. You're the surfer, riding the waves of change. It's not about pretending that we always experience positive emotions and thoughts. Negative ones are equally natural and human, and it's harmful to deny yourself the experience of such emotions. The goal of this chapter is to develop ways to deal with what often makes us feel bad, how we can accept these feelings and how we can best live with them. The reward for this is huge – it might be the most important step of this book for you.

Sigmund Freud, the founder of psychoanalysis, said we are governed by the 'pleasure principle' which is our instinct to seek pleasures and avoid pain. I predict that this will be the hardest step to happiness in this book. It has certainly been the hardest for me (and still is), and I know many people who struggle with it.

Your unconscious mind is filled with fears and past worries that you've never faced or attempted to heal. They've been slumbering in the comfortable back of your mind, dragging you down time and time again. We could even question the commonly used phrase, *time heals all wounds,* because just letting time pass does not address the festering wound. You still need to attend to your wound and clean it for it to start healing. When emotional pain is bottled up, it can lead to bitterness, unexplained low moods, and isolation later down the line. People often say *a clean home is a happy home.* Since many of us spend much of our time living in our minds, we better start putting things in a little more order. It's time to clean our mental home.

If you're anything like I used to be, you will be tempted to skip this chapter and move on to lighter pages of the book. It's hard work to face our emotional pain and fears. It's much more comfortable just to ignore and avoid it all. *You're surviving right now, why risk it? Why not just keep it as it is?*

How often do you distract yourself when negative feelings come up? Do you drink or blast music to silence your pain? Our parents or teachers never taught us how to deal with emotional pain. We don't have the tools or reassurance that we'll be okay if we try to do so. I want you to know that you will be okay. Even if you experience hurt, you will be okay. I promise you that.

It can be a good idea to seek a coach or therapist to guide you further - especially if you're healing from deeper traumas. My good friend, Olly Sheehan is a mind coach and NLP practitioner. He specialises in helping people deal with their emotions and understanding the processes of the unconscious mind. Olly can be a key resource for you if you would like more support and personal guidance in a one to one coaching setting. There's also plenty of other amazing coaches and therapist online or in your local area.

Learning to deal with emotions, especially those we often deem as negative, is something you will have to work on sooner or later. If you decide to skip this step, you will have to come back to it one day. There's no running away. It's best to lay the foundations now! The benefits of facing your emotions are enormous. You will become a stronger, more resilient and a happier person as a result.

Start cleaning that wound so it can start healing. We got this!

Do Not Use Distractions

There will be times when it's okay to use moderate distractions, especially if a situation is too overwhelming. I still distract myself from time to time. Sometimes, it's better to step out of it than to let your thoughts spiral and amplify the emotion beyond control. As you develop your skill of facing pain and emotions, try to avoid silencing them as much as possible.

If unattended, the wound will fester. Even if you blast your music or neck a few bottles of beer. Instead, embrace the potential for silence around you. Embrace what comes up. Be curious. Face it, feel it and heal it. That, my dear friends, is the best way to tackle the pain associated with negative emotions (this is not the end of the chapter!)

It's damn hard at times but silence is crucial in the process. Instead of creating noise to distract your mind, try to create a silent setting. Noise cancelling headphones are an ironic term if you think about it, right? What about the noise inside the headphones?

Enjoy the natural calm around you. What initially helped me to create silence was lighting some candles, turning my phone on flight mode and reading a book or cleaning my house. You don't need to become an enlightened master or spend all your day in silence. A few minutes a day is fine. Fall in love with those quiet moments; they hold the key to transformation! Your body and mind communicate with you naturally and this is the time to truly listen. Become aware of what's going on without all the distractions. As Martin Luther King said, "only light can drive out darkness" and you need to give yourself the space to let light in. In the beginning, a few rays is totally fine. Later on, you'll be sunbathing 😊.

Science Says; Don't Suppress Your Negative Emotions!

The scientific evidence is clear, suppressing negative emotions is a terrible idea. In *The Happiness Track: How to Apply the Science of Happiness to Accelerate Your Success*, Emma Seppala draws on research from Stanford University, finding that people who suppressed negative emotions generally experienced more of them. That should be a wake-up call for many of us. You can browse study after study, they mostly come to a similar conclusion: don't suppress your feelings.

Negative Emotions Can Benefit You

When I first started to learn about happiness, all I wanted was to surround myself with positive feelings. If I felt guilty or sad, I would try to push it away. I soon realised that my initial instinct was wrong! I discovered that you can live a fulfilled life *and* experience emotional pains at the same time. In fact, negative emotions that evoke a painful reaction in us have an essential role to play. By rejecting anything that wasn't making me feel amazing, I was missing out on a valuable part of life.

Negative emotions help to ensure you stay on track. They are like your compass. Guilt, embarrassment, fear, and sadness all have an important role to play in our lives. Imagine you never felt guilty - you would be one mean human being. The feeling of guilt, although painful, is useful in ensuring we act morally well and treat others with dignity. If we never feel bad about how we might have intentionally or unintentionally mistreated people, we would destroy all our relationships.

Imagine you never felt embarrassed - you might only walk around in ripped t-shirts and dirty joggers, even at business meetings. Your chances of landing a new client that will help to pay for your family's needs and survival are vastly lowered. Imagine you never felt regret - you would miss out on many more future opportunities. Imagine you never felt fear - you would get yourself into a ton of trouble. Imagine you never felt sadness - what would joy be without its sister, sadness? Your joyful moments would be far less special.

We need to use these so-called negative emotions to our advantage whenever possible. They are the compass to guide you. See them as tools to strengthen your relationships and ways to explore yourself better.

In terms of personal growth, the experience of pain allows us to shine a light on areas that require more of our focus. Pain reveals to you what you still need to learn and work on. It's never a good idea to brush off pain and move on. You need to first embrace and attend to the pain. Try to listen to it and allow it to be your teacher.

"Man is a pupil, pain is his teacher."
Alfred de Musset

Accept Your Darkside

No, this is not an invitation to join the dark side. I'm suggesting that we shouldn't be so fearful or ashamed of our dark side. We must accept it. *Felix, wait. Are you saying I have a dark side?* Yes, you do. We all do, we just hate to admit it!

Resisting our dark side and holding on to the image of ourselves as an angelic being can often evoke feelings of guilt and sadness. Once we have accepted that we have evolutionary desires of survival and greed which can make us manipulative, selfish and harsh at times, we are then ready to make changes in our life for the better! As Robert Biswas-Diener and Todd Kashdan write in their book, *The Upside of the Dark Side*, the goal should be to strive not just for happiness but for 'wholeness' which includes embracing our dark side.

Childhood and the Past

As children, we used to create maps in our mind to make sense of this crazy place called Earth! We might have formed a belief that the world is a scary place if we experienced some fear-inducing events when playing outside. A victim mindset is also something many of us carry with us into adulthood from the mental maps we drew as children. As a child, it was harder to change situations. It was harder to walk away from friends and family who might be causing us pain. It was harder to tell your brother Billy that you need a few weeks break from seeing him because he's annoying. It's important to realise that this is no longer the case.

You now have a say on many aspects of your life. To further conquer this victim-mindset, one thing you can always control is the way you respond.

For people who experienced or witnessed violence or highly traumatic events in childhood, the impacts of such meaning maps might be worse, but it affects *all* of us to some degree.

Emotions are also a record of the past. Suppressed emotions are stored in the body, especially those generated from traumatic events. The unconscious mind stores all memories from the past and this is what Eckhart Tolle and other teachers have called *the pain body*. When you over-react to an unjustified emotion, your pain body is triggered. Many of them are stored in our body from past events and can easily resurface. Whenever I over-react, it's immensely helpful that I can recognise the source. *Oh hey, that's the pain body coming alive again.* This simple awareness helps calm me down and detaches me from the situation a little. It helps me regain some control over my mind.

To heal from emotions stored in our body, it's crucial to work through these emotions. This will make space for more positive feelings to enter your life.

Two Helpful Terms

Your State: Your state is how you feel before, during and after an emotion. It can be particularly helpful to bring awareness to the state you were in before you experienced the emotion. Did you have a stressful day? Did you skip breakfast? All of this could have contributed to your response. Feel your state during the emotion. Is your body tensing up? How about after the emotion, how are you feeling now? Can you avoid letting the emotion become uncontrollable? Shine the light of awareness on it all.

Trigger: Emotions and memories are stored in our body and unconscious mind. These are often associated with sensory perceptions and memories of the past like smells, sounds, visuals, touch, and places. Have you noticed how songs you listened to when you were in a joyful time of your life, instantly make you happy when you hear them? This is called a trigger. When you see someone who caused you pain, this can trigger you into feeling bad. Become aware of triggers to help you realise that the negative feeling has a direct cause. No need to blame yourself.

The Atlas of Emotions

Have you heard of the *Atlas of Emotions*? It's a legendary piece of work resulting from a survey of 149 scientists. Psychologist Dr.Paul Ekman, his daughter Dr.Eve Ekman and the Dalai Lama himself created the Atlas of Emotions. The map sorts emotions into five main groups. *Anger, Disgust, Sadness, Fear, Enjoyment.*

Often, we might be unclear about the trigger, state or actual emotion we are experiencing. With the map, we can clearly investigate what it is and start healing ourselves from stored emotions.

Disentangle Emotions From Thoughts (and vice versa)

Your thoughts fuel your emotions and your emotions fuel your thoughts. It works both ways. When an emotion is causing you pain, your thoughts might add more pain to this feeling. As clinical psychologist Dr.Jordan Peterson said in a recent interview, "it's key to disentangle thoughts from emotions". Just as thoughts come and go, emotions work the same way. They only seem as if they last for so long because we focus on them and fuse thoughts and emotions together. To reiterate, what we experience is not the problem, the problem is how we respond!

How can we approach letting go of the pain associated with anger?

In the *Atlas of Emotions*, anger is seen as a primary emotion. If we dive deeper, we can often find fear or sadness at the root of anger. We often choose anger over fear or sadness because responding in anger makes us feel less vulnerable and more in control. The goal should always be to bring awareness to the primary emotion, it's the most effective way to dissolve it.

Let's say you might be angry at your boss for cutting your hours. At the root of your anger is fear for your job security. You're angry at your boss because you fear for your livelihood. Bring awareness to the primary emotion. Since adopting this approach, I've started to feel like a detective trying to uncover the root of the emotions I'm feeling. It's tough but it's also quite intriguing.

The feeling of fear in your body is far from pleasant to face, but it won't seriously harm you. The emotion will not suddenly disappear but if you approach it with acceptance, you can start to disentangle the link between emotions and thoughts and begin to let go of pain. Awareness is key. When we feel an emotion rising, it feels as if it has a tight grip around our ability to think or act rationally. You could try shouting - *Oi, emotion, let go of me!* ...but it won't help very much. If anything, the grip will get tighter.

With awareness, you become aware that the emotion is not YOU. With this perspective, you will already be in a better place to act rationally. The emotion will start to loosen its grip. Additionally, you might choose to remove yourself from a situation entirely to give yourself some time to calm down. Awareness is always better than the tight grip the emotion has on you. It's much kinder to your vocal cords than shouting!

It's crucial that we don't try to explain everything with logic. Just feel and accept what you are feeling in your body. Our over-reliance on logic sometimes works against us when we can't make sense of certain feelings and sensations.

Question Your Thoughts

Noah Elkin argues that one trick to happiness is not to believe your thoughts. Believing thoughts results in the creation of emotion and attachment to negative beliefs.

How do you take a step back and stop believing your thoughts?

You question them. You question their validity. *Is it true that everyone thinks my presentation sucked? Do I know that for a fact? I guess I don't know for sure. Let me drop this thought then.* By doing so, you'll break the link before negative emotions can creep into your life. Noah argues that if you stop believing what makes you unhappy, you will be left with happiness. Have a go at this. It requires little theory but plenty of practise.

MBCT – Mindfulness is Key!

Who remembers what MBCT stands for? Yes, nice one - Mindfulness-Based Cognitive Therapy. In this busy world, we can all do with some of this peaceful yet effective therapy. We need to get away from the idea that engaging in therapy means there is something wrong with us. It's a way of showing how much we care about ourselves and our well-being.

Become aware of sensations in your body. This is key to face your emotions and all that is stored in the unconscious mind. We often think we have no say over our reaction to thoughts and feelings; MBCT shows us this is far from the truth.

The point of view of awareness we use to observe our thoughts and emotions is incredibly peaceful. If you're not sure what I mean, you will experience it when you practise meditation. If we can tap into this awareness some more and associate less with our thoughts, then we can also live more peacefully. Just as with the *outsider's view*, when you observe emotions, acknowledge them and shine a light of awareness on them. They'll behave much better as a result!

I know everyone is saying *meditate, meditate, meditate* as if it was the cure for everything - it isn't. However, meditation can really help with accepting and dealing with fears and emotions. There are so many amazing guided meditations out there that leave you feeling refreshed and in control of your life.

It's also a good idea to find some meditations that focus on the heart. We all need to take a little more care of our heart, it's doing a tremendous job. Try to breathe in through your nose and visualise the air and new energy flowing into your heart. This type of meditation can help release tension and free your heart space (sometimes called heart-chakra). What all this boils down to is awareness (surprise, surprise). Be aware of your emotions and you can respond much more appropriately in the moment, or start the healing process for emotions stored in your unconscious mind.

Face Your Fears

"The key to change... is to let go of fear."
Rosanne Cash

You might have noticed that this chapter has *Face your Fears* in the title. So far, we've pretty much only talked about emotions and Star Wars references of embracing your dark side. Yet, what we've covered so far encapsulates what most of us fear the most - facing how we feel inside. In music or other art forms, you'll often find people expressing that they have demons in them they're too fearful to face. Generic song lyric: *Be mine and hold me, because I have demons, I'm too scared to face when I'm alone.*

Whatever you are fearful of, you need to feel it and experience it in the present moment. The reward will be a vastly more blissful life. If you never immerse yourself in what you're fearful of, you will miss out on living a fulfilled life and doing things you want to do. The act of avoiding what scares you has become normal behaviour for most of us. I've been stuck in that way of living more than I'd like to admit. I try to avoid it as much as I can these days. I hope I can motivate you to do the same.

In the present moment, there is no fear because fear is based on thoughts. Fear is a prediction your mind forms about what you think will happen next. Never about what is actually happening right now. Become aware of your fears. What's scaring you? The unknown is almost always scarier than the matter itself once you're aware of it. Ask yourself what is *actually* scaring you.

I saw a role model of mine post a question on social media asking, 'What gets in the way of your happiness?' Over 80% of people said fear. This demonstrated to me how important it is for us to tackle fear face on.

There's good news and bad news when it comes to fear. The bad news is you can never fully get rid of it. The good news is that anyone can take steps to decrease their fear.

You decrease fear by:
- Becoming aware of what you fear.
- Repeatedly exposing yourself to what you fear.

> *"The only thing we have to fear, is fear itself."*
> **Franklin D. Roosevelt**

There's No 'Quick Fix' - Let's Take A Walk in The Forest of Life

Just like *My Happiness Button* is not a quick fix solution, facing your fears and emotions is not a quick fix either. When something troubling comes up, you can use the methods you've discovered in this chapter. You cannot, however, free yourself all at once. If you've spent years entertaining pain, you need to be kind to yourself and give yourself some time to heal. You are on the right path. Imagine this path takes us to a forest. The forest of life.

You're blindfolded and walking through a forest. You can't take off the blindfold because you've had it on for so long. The sunlight would make you go blind in seconds. The forest symbolises your life. The trees symbolise your negative emotions. The blindfold symbolises all the things you've used to hide from your emotions.

Right now, you're in a deserted part of the forest. There's not many resources here. No fresh berries to eat or water to drink. All the abundant resources are in the northern part of the forest. You're very hungry and thirsty. If you want to stay alive, you have no choice but to move forward. You move towards the north of the forest. Everything seems to be going fine for a few minutes and you think to yourself, "Oh this isn't so bad I've walked quite a bit without any trouble". It's only a matter of time until you walk into a tree and hurt yourself. "Ouch! Where did that come from? Why is it always me that gets hurt?"

*Along the path, you step on a book. You pick it up and go into a cave, away from the sunlight. You get out a small torch to read what's written. The book seems to be a book on dealing with emotions. It says **Learn to face your emotions and become mindful of how they make you feel**. Knowing that you have nothing to lose, you give this technique a go. You discover that when applying this technique, your eyes begin to naturally heal themselves to allow more light and blissfulness into your life. You're able to slowly lift the blindfold. You discover that you're able to look directly at the trees. You even run your hand across the tree bark. Feel it. Become aware of it. Feel how your eyes strengthen with every tree you mindfully embrace.*

You proceed north at a steady pace, feeling more at ease with every step. In the denser part of the forest, fallen trees get in the way of your path. You think you will be unable to proceed on your journey towards the north. Your new sense of self-compassion and complete acceptance of the forest and all its trees allows you to take a step back. You observe the fallen trees for what they are. You feel everything they make you feel. Sadness that your journey might end here. Anger that this tree is blocking your way. Guilt that you might never see your family again. Shame for your behaviour in the past that led you here. You feel and embrace it all. As you observe the trees, your eyesight strengthens some more. You start to notice a small gap between the fallen trees. You climb through it and joyfully proceed towards the abundant parts of the forest. You have no doubt in your mind that whatever happens in the forest, you will be able to deal with it with your new sense of awareness, acceptance, and compassion. Finally, you reach the north of the forest and reunite with your family. They point out how they don't recognise you. They say that you've changed into a beautiful and kind human being. You tell them that you didn't change, you just uncovered your true self. You notice that although less dense, there are still trees in the northern part of the forest. The only difference is that you now no longer need your blindfold, and you have a mindful approach to the forest and its trees. Life is amazing.

Try to keep this analogy in mind as you go about your life. When you find yourself using an escape from your negative emotions, ask yourself, *do I want to wear that blindfold? Do I want to keep running into trees and hurting myself?* Or *do I want to see the trees clearly, accepting them as part of the forest? Do I want to reach the abundant lands with tasty berries and fresh water?* The choice is yours.

Steps to Happiness via Face Your Fears & Negative Emotions

FEEL EMOTIONS IN YOUR BODY. EXPRESS LOVE AND LET GO

Becoming aware of feelings in your body and expressing love towards them is arguably the most effective method out there. It works for newly experienced emotions but also tackles past traumas stored in your body. Here's a five-step guide.

1. Use the body scan. Sitting or lying down, close your eyes. Start with your feet and scan each part of your body mentally, feeling all the sensations. Sit with each part for some time and bring awareness to it. You can do this without guidance or with guided meditation via *YouTube* or an app.

2. Bring to mind an event that made you feel a particular emotion or focus on how you're feeling now. If you're unsure about how you felt during an event, bring up the event and see what

feelings and sensations appear. Scan your body again, paying close attention to any sensations. It might be tightness in your shoulders or a stiff neck. If possible, mentally note what kind of sensations you're feeling. Try to be as detailed and aware as possible. This technique is key for understanding and shining a light on emotions and past events.

3. Now that you have become clearer of what the sensation feels like and what emotion it's associated with, express love for everything you feel in that moment. This step is key for acceptance and letting go. *I love you sadness. I am human, so it is normal for me to feel sad. You're part of the compass guiding my life.*

4. Continue to fully feel the emotion and sensations in your body without suppressing or denying yourself any part of the experience. Explore it. Accept it. Take on a loving and kind attitude towards it. If you feel like crying, allow yourself to cry. If you feel empowered and want to release a cheer, do that! If you just want to scream and release tension, then grab a pillow and let it all out. Screaming and using your voice to release can be a powerful way to bring out emotions hiding in your unconscious. Be mindful of what comes up. Screaming always makes you feel lighter afterwards.

5. At the end of your session, imagine letting go of your pain. You could imagine placing your pain inside a suitcase and leaving it behind as you walk on a new path to a lighter and more blissful future. Guided meditations will usually have their own way of helping you let go at the end of your session.

START TACKLING TROUBLING CHILDHOOD NARRATIVE

Memories, traumatic events and the way we were raised have a profound impact on how we experience life today. To tackle the root cause of emotional traumas, it's crucial to work with childhood memories. Daniel Siegel, the author of *Mindsight* suggests writing down your earliest memories. Bringing awareness to them will help to reduce the impact they have on your unconscious mind.

A POWERFUL EXERCISE IS WRITING A LETTER FOR CLOSURE.

With this technique, you can receive the apology you never received but is crucial for your well-being and peace of mind. To achieve a sense of closure, it can help to role-play an exchange. Be as detailed and raw as you like. Then, write a second letter as a response to your first one. Be as detailed as possible and draw on anything you feel might get you closure.

What do you need to hear to start healing? You could even write this letter to a family member if you have a difficult relationship with them. There are no limits to who you can write to and how often you can write this letter. It might take a few letters to finally give you a sense of relief.

PUT YOUR NEGATIVE EMOTIONS INTO WORDS

As Shawn Achor mentions in *The Happiness Advantage*, brain scans have shown that putting negative emotions into words reduces their power! You don't need a brain scan to prove this in your own life. Nine times out of ten, when you write down or talk about a negative emotion, you feel better. As a musician, I can relate to that. It can be very therapeutic to translate my emotions into lyrics. It's almost cleansing. We all want to feel like someone is listening. When I record, I visualise a crowd of people listening to my voice. It's how I let off steam. It's part of how I feel heard.

QUESTION YOUR THOUGHTS

When you keep questioning the thought, you find that most of your worries and anxieties are merely based on suspicions. A situation might not be as bad as you think. It might even be for the better. Most likely, you don't know if it will be good or bad, so why assume it will be bad? Stay curious.

IS IT REALLY SO NEGATIVE?

Accepting and seeing the positive in all situations, without denying any feelings, is crucial! Remember that pain and so-called negative emotions are teachers that help you correct your behaviour and become the best version of yourself.

TAKE OWNERSHIP

No matter how other people have acted towards you, they did not *make* you feel in any way. If you're annoyed, it's because *you* created that response. Take ownership for how you're feeling and get out of the victim mentality! This is not about suppressing negative emotions, it's about taking ownership of how you feel and fully feeling what is present in your life.

TALK IT OUT

To disentangle thoughts from emotions, it's important to speak to someone. It's harder to do it just in your mind. This could be a friend, therapist or mentor. If you want to face strong emotions, I would always recommend a therapist as your friends might end up feeling overwhelmed and might confuse you. You could also try journaling to talk it out with yourself. Although, this should be an addition, not a substitute for talking to real people.

WHY?!

There are very few words in the English language that are as emotionally charged as the word *why*. Whichever language you choose, the equivalent of *why* will be an emotionally loaded word. If you feel that you have a lot of emotional weight on you, try getting in front of the mirror and saying the word *why* over, and over again. You might look a little crazy so consider finding a peaceful spot so you can let out as many *whys* as you need. With every *why*, you'll be releasing some emotional tension.

You might even find yourself crying for no reason. I certainly did at first. You're directly tapping into stored emotions in the unconscious mind and releasing the sadness or guilt stored within you. This exercise works wonders. Sometimes crying is exactly what we need. You will feel much lighter after the exercise. Remember if you need to scream, grab that pillow!

DEEEP BREATHING!

When you change your breathing, you can also change your emotional state. Luckily, we can control our breath and reap the benefits of deep and slow breathing. You can often spot me breathing deeply, even in public! War veterans suffering from post-traumatic stress disorder (PTSD) have found much help by breathing slowly and deeply. Slower breathing has shown to reduce cortisol (the stress hormone) in our body.

Take 10 minutes a day to breathe deeply and slowly. Especially in emotional situations, try to incorporate deep breaths to reduce stress and increase that feeling of calm within you. You can always control your breathing, that's the power of the breath.

MOVEMENT AND STRETCHES TO RELEASE

Emotional pain does not come in isolation. Often physical symptoms are a consequence of emotional suffering. Areas of the body that are often associated with emotional pain are the jaw, chest, stomach/solar plexus, the neck, and hip area. With heartbreak especially, you might be feeling tightness in the chest.

When you start moving, this fuels the flowing of energy in your body. Get in motion to release emotion. This could be going for a walk, run or swim. Stuck energies are never a good idea. Get energies to flow more freely in your body by getting active.

If you want something that is directly targeted at releasing pent-up emotions in the body, you can do some focused stretches that help to release the tensions associated with emotional pain. Yoga is an ancient and common form of releasing physical tensions. You can find many exercises online or consult a yoga teacher. You don't need to join yoga classes to release trapped energy, you can easily do it from the comfort of your home.

The hip area is a common area that tenses up in times of stress as our body activates and then suppresses the fight or flight response. There are many 'hip-openers' you can do to release emotional tension. Just give them a quick google search. The importance of the jaw is also often overlooked! The jaw is a sensitive stress sensor that can become tense when we're dealing with a busy lifestyle and difficult emotions. With jaw yoga, you can release these tensions. I'm part of the team who invented the term and created an app with many useful jaw relaxation exercises: visit Kieferfreund.com - German for *Jaw Friend*.

Don't underestimate the mind-body connection. Stretch and take care of your body to deal with emotions effectively.

FASTER EFT TAPPING – TAP YOUR WAY TO BLISS!

No, this isn't an Irish folk dance. It's an alternative method to tackle emotional pain, anxiety and stress effectively. I'm not an expert on it but I want to make you aware of it. Many people have reported that it worked for them when all else failed. EFT stands for Emotional Focused Transformation. It's a method we can use to re-structure the pathways in our brain by tapping on specific points on our body that are connected to our fight or flight response. This method directly impacts the mind and body connection, influencing how thoughts and emotions impact our body. The tapping method helps to ground us and break this link. A few of the points used are temples, collarbone and wrist. Faster EFT is a method developed by American therapist, Robert Smith who combined what he learned from NLP (Neuro-linguistic programming) and traditional EFT to create Faster EFT. Robert takes a very scientific approach, and this has allowed his method to be accepted in schools and many other institutions.

USE AFFIRMATIONS

Affirmations such *as It's okay, I have overcome difficult situations before, I can do it now too* are powerful to keep you on course. Simple as that.

SELF-COMPASSION & COMPASSION

In *Emotional Agility*, Dr.Susan David says self-compassion is the best way to tame negative emotions. Recognise and listen to your emotions. Susan suggests a simple exercise of bringing to mind the child you once were. This child is still in you today. Accept who you are and see your flaws with compassion. Don't be so hard on yourself! No need to judge so heavily. We're all in this together. Dissolve the notion of separateness. **puff**

KEEP THE FOREST ANALOGY IN MIND

Do you want to be blindfolded and constantly bump into trees or will you strengthen your eye-sight and awareness? Get yourself to those damn tasty berries, fresh water, and your loved ones.

OBJECTIFY YOUR EMOTION

Although objectifying people is a no-go, objectifying emotions is perfectly fine. In one of the best TEDx talks I've ever seen, *Why You Feel What You Feel*, Alan Watkins suggests objectifying the emotions we experience. This means stepping back and saying *oh, this is anger* or *oh, this is joy*. Once we take this step, then we will be able to navigate through our emotional landscape, identifying what it is we are feeling and loosening the grip it has on us. At the end of his talk, Alan says a key phrase, "If you can control your emotions, you can change your life completely." Let's use this phrase to motivate us!

GROUND YOURSELF WITH A COMFORTING OBJECT

In my podcast *The Felix New Show*, I invited one of my Instagram followers to join me on the podcast to talk about self-care. The lovely Manisha, who's originally from India and currently lives in the States, mentioned a highly effective tool. In her work with victims of violence and abuse, Manisha sometimes holds on to a shell to ground herself when hearing about difficult stories. Find the object that comforts and grounds you. An object from nature is usually the most calming and powerful.

TAKE WELL-DESERVED BREAKS

I know I said you shouldn't practise escapism but if you approach it with the intention to take a break and to gather strength, then I think it's highly advisable to practise activities that fulfil and excite you. Doing what you enjoy re-charges you and takes your mind off things. Only *you* know how often you need breaks. Feel free to take them. Be kind to yourself. Become a good friend to yourself.

FACE YOUR FEARS

The 5 Second Rule

Mel Robbins's book, *The 5 Second Rule: Transform Your Life, Work, and Confidence with Everyday Courage* teaches us a straightforward trick to conquer the fear stopping us from doing the things we would like to do.

If you're scared to ask your boss for a promotion but you know it's something you need in order to progress in your career then you count down from 5 and GO.

5,4,3,2,1 and GO!

You don't give fearful thoughts the chance to creep into your head. If there's something you want to do, just count down and do it. The method really works. I use it in the mornings every time I'm fearful of how cold it'll be when I get out of bed.

Engage with Your Fears as with Emotions

Many of the steps for facing 'negative' emotions can equally be used for facing what scares you. The body scan works well, and also talking to someone or writing things down work wonders to dissolve the fear. Writing down how something makes you feel, can sometimes be less overwhelming than thinking about it in your head and could be useful to take another perspective on your fear. Taking the fear out of your mind and on to paper gives you a new perspective and sense of detachment from it all.

Find Out Exactly What Your Fear Is

The unknown is usually scarier than the event itself. Not knowing exactly what you're scared of lets your mind run free to map out thousands of possible scenarios. Get crystal clear about what scares you. Keep asking *what* and *why* questions. Tackle the unknown. Make it show itself. Once you are crystal clear, it will be less scary.

Rationalise Your Thoughts

You might be clear about what's scaring you. You might even be clear about the emotion this fear generates in you. Now, ask yourself how likely is it that things will happen as I imagine them? Similar to Noah's method of questioning your thoughts, try to understand that it's highly unlikely that what you fear will play out exactly as you imagine it. Fear is often merely *false evidence appearing real.*

Love Your Fear

Fear is your friend because it will help you grow. When you surrender to the moment and get out of your head, your adrenalin will kick in to ensure you deliver the best possible version of yourself. Love your fear.

Equally, when fear creeps in to remind you to earn enough money to pay the rent then it's a helpful supporter. Imagine if you never got these reminders. You'd be screwed. Accept and love your fear as part of your experience yet recognise that you are not your fear. You are simply the awareness behind the fear. Next time you feel fearful, try saying to yourself *I love you fear* and observe what it does for you.

Be Present with Your Fear

In the present moment, your fears will evaporate. Fear is speculation about potential future events. When you're present, your fears will fall apart in front of your eyes and you can take the best possible action. You will act from a place of love, not fear. That's a winning recipe.

Face Your Fears: Do Something That Scares You Every Day

Right next to my bed is a small, paper note reading the words *do something today that scares you!* My goal is to face my fears at least once a day. This builds massive momentum and yields amazing results in my life. Remember, if you don't regularly expose yourself to fear, you will lose the benefits of being courageous. It's a muscle you must continue to train.

"Forget Everything and Run, or, Face Everything and Rise. The choice is yours."

Zig Ziglar

IN A NUTSHELL

- The problem is never how we feel or what we think, but the way we respond!
- There is no such thing as negative. Good and bad are mental constructs.
- *"Face it, feel it and heal it"*
- We shouldn't deny ourselves negative emotions, they're part of our experience and need to be felt fully.
- So-called negative emotions help you stay on course in life and can benefit you.

- When emotional pain is bottled up instead of faced, it can lead to bitterness, unexplained low moods and isolation.

- As we are governed by Freud's 'pleasure principle', it can be hard to face our emotional pain and fears.

- We were never really taught how to deal with emotions, but you will be *okay* when trying to face them.

- You can't run away from your pent-up emotions. They will show themselves again and again until you step up and face them.

- Facing emotions can be challenging and working with a therapist can be helpful and effective.

- Do not use distractions to silence emotions. You should allow yourself to take breaks when needed out of self-care.

- Scientific evidence clearly states the importance of not suppressing our emotions and instead, bringing awareness to them.

- Pain is a crucial teacher in life.

- Accept your dark side and strive for 'wholeness'.

- Much of the emotional suffering you face today stems from the past.

- Disentangling thoughts and emotions is key.

- The *Atlas of Emotions* is one bad-ass resource.

- Try to be aware of your state before, during and after experiencing an emotion as these impact your experience. Equally, watch out for triggers.

- Mindfulness and awareness are the keys for an emotionally balanced life.

- Facing negative emotions is no quick fix. It takes time.

- Tensions in the body are often manifestations of unfaced emotions.

- Fear often gets in the way of our happiness.

- In the present moment, there is no fear.

- What we fear is often the unknown.

- Could there also be positives arising from a situation that scares you? Will you grow as a result? Will it be a blessing in disguise?

- Fear will never leave you but with repeated exposure, you can become less fearful.

- It's a mental muscle you must train to maintain.

SUMMARY OF STEPS

Face Your Negative Emotions

1. Feel Emotions in Your Body. Express Love and Let Go
2. Start Tackling Troubling Childhood Narrative
3. Put Your Negative Emotions into Words
4. Question Your Thoughts
5. Is it Really so Negative?
6. Take Ownership
7. Talk it Out
8. WHY?!
9. Deeep Breathing!
10. Movement and Stretches to Release
11. Faster EFT Tapping – Tap your Way to Bliss!
12. Use Affirmations
13. Self-compassion & Compassion
14. Keep the Forest Analogy in Mind
15. Objectify Your Emotion
16. Ground Yourself with a Comforting Object
17. Take Well-deserved Breaks

Face Your Fears

1. The 5 Second Rule
2. Engage with Your Fears as with Emotions
3. Find Out Exactly What Your Fear is

4. Rationalise Your Thoughts

5. Love Your Fear

6. Be Present with Your Fear

7. Face Your Fears: Do Something That Scares You Every Day

--------------------- Please read ---------------------
A Final Note from Felix New

The techniques you've learned in this chapter will take away the unconscious baggage of emotions and feelings that might have been dragging you down. It can be painful and difficult at times, so I understand if maybe you are not terribly keen to jump in head-first. Start with doing some work on the surface. By doing meditations, you can work on becoming more mindful of your emotions and thoughts in the moment. Be sure to shine the light of awareness on what you're experiencing. In terms of diving deeper, you need to trust yourself to know when you're ready. On a recent podcast, my good friend Frankie Cote says your mind knows when you're strong enough to start facing what is stored deep in your unconscious. The focus is on strengthening yourself with the other chapters in this book and becoming more mindful of all that is going on, within and around you. You will know when you're ready to dive deeper. Once you do, you will change your life in the most beautiful and powerful way. If you need a therapist or coach to support you, that's totally fine too. I always say this and it's so true - *baby steps are steps too.* This can be a long process, but never give up. It's time to rise and shine.

ADDITIONAL RESOURCES

Mind Coach Olly Sheehan: https://www.ollysheehan.com/

The Atlas of Emotions: You can find the *Atlas of Emotions* here http://atlasofemotions.org.

Meditations: A recent one I discovered is by entrepreneur and speaker Eric Ho, who has shared stages with the likes of Richard Branson. You can find it on *YouTube*: 'Eric Ho - Most Powerful guided meditation for letting go'. In the meditation, Eric guides us to visualise things we are struggling to let go in order to feel the emotions attached to it. Then, he uses the numbers 10-1 to dial down our attachment to them. He uses terms such as *third eye* and *chakra* but if this is unfamiliar to you, don't worry. This meditation will still work. Just give it a go!

Movement and Stretches: Another good resource is Dr.David Berceli. He's written a book called *Shake It Off Naturally*. David shows us trauma releasing exercises or *TRE* for short. It can take a long time to release pent-up emotions with exercises. However, once you've 'shaken them off', it's liberating to say the least!

CHAPTER 10: ADDITIONAL STEPS TO HAPPINESS

Additional Steps – Elevating Your Happiness

The main chapters of this book help you to develop your *internal* force of happiness. This chapter is focused on the *external* steps you can take to elevate and boost the happiness you've started to nurture.

To practise internal happiness effectively and peacefully, it's crucial that you also cultivate a healthy environment around you. Many of these steps have been absolutely life-changing for me.

Be Mindful of Who You Spend Time With

The Importance of Close Social Relationships

In many blogs, articles, and books, you'll find people saying that close relationships are important for long-term happiness. These relationships help us deal with the ups and downs of life and keep us mentally and physically sharp. Happiness is found in the experience of positive emotions and that is exactly what happens when you spend quality time with people. You feel good. When spending time with loved ones, your body releases the hormone oxytocin, which makes you feel happy and secure. Anxiety is also reduced. In close and functional social relationships, you care for each other, listen to each other and give each other a sense of assurance and trust. These qualities are vital contributors to a happier life.

Unfortunately, many of us struggle to maintain close relationships. A recent report by the Red Cross and Co-op found that over 9 million people in the UK are always or often lonely. The report found that loneliness has a serious impact on our health and doesn't just affect older people. Loneliness is said to increase the risk of mortality by 26%!

It's crucial that we work on our relationships and aim to reduce loneliness. It's not about accumulating as many Facebook friends as possible. It's about creating meaningful relationships. Quality and depth > quantity.

It's time for the Okinawans to make another appearance. Supposedly some of the happiest folk alive, most Okinawans have a strong social network of lifelong friends. The term they use for this group is *Moai* which translates to 'meeting for a common purpose'. The purpose of these support groups is to provide financial, health, social and even spiritual support. I'd love to have *Moai*'s in the UK. It would be life changing for so many people suffering from loneliness.

Build a Community – Build Your Ark

When you have the intention to form closer relationships with people and you work on yourself to bring great qualities to the table, your natural instincts will do a lot of the work for you and you'll soon attract like-minded people. It won't be easy, but it will be worth it. Bring to the table what you expect others to bring. If you already have a pretty decent community of close social relationships, then aim to become even closer to the people in your network. Give them your undivided attention. Put that phone down! Think of it as your own version of Noah's Ark. Get people on board your ship to navigate the ocean of life and waves of change.

Filter Out Toxic People (and surround yourself with positive ones)

"You are the average of the five people you spend the most time with."
Jim Rohn

Behaviour rubs off on you. People who are often in a bad mood and have a negative approach to life will make you feel more negative and less confident. People who are positive and generally in a good mood will uplift and inspire you.

People who have a negative attitude aren't bad people, but they still have a long way to go to work on themselves. You don't have time to let them drag you down. Don't hate them but don't spend your time around them either. These people could be in your close environment which makes cutting them off more difficult. They might be a family member, a co-worker or friend you've had since childhood. Try to minimise the time you spend with them. If it's your parents, move out when you can. If it's your partner, maybe it's time to re-think your relationship. You don't need to filter everyone out from one day to the next but be determined to step out of 'toxic' relationships as soon as possible. How long would you take to treat a toxic spider bite? Probably not very long.

Spend as much time as possible around positive people! Spending more time around like-minded and positive people will make you feel alive and happy like never before. It will make you realise why we are social beings – we need each other.

Make a list. Put down all the people you spend most of your time with. Sort them into 'happiness depleters' and 'happiness boosters'. Start filtering. Start surrounding yourself with positive people. Watch your life and happiness change.

DON'T FORGET THE MIND-BODY CONNECTION

Move Your Body

Exercise is immensely powerful when it comes to boosting your mood and making you feel happy. Your body releases endorphins and serotonin (feel-good hormones) when you exercise and regulates adrenalin levels (stress hormone). Exercise boosts your happiness and energy levels. With a stronger immune system, you'll also reduce the risk of illness.

According to a recent article from Harvard Health Publishing, sustained low-intensity exercise allows nerve cells in our bodies to grow and improve the way our brain works! The hippocampus, the part of our brain responsible for our mood is said to grow in those who exercise regularly. Studies have even shown that exercise is one of the best cures for mild to moderate depression! The NHS recommends that adults do 150 minutes of moderately intense exercise a week.

What Are You Putting into Your Body?!

There are so many different diets out there that promise to be the path to good health. I'm not going to endorse any of them because I believe there's no one-fits-all solution when it comes to what we eat.

Due to the crucial mind-body connection, it can boost your happiness if you find the optimal diet for your body. For me, increasing plant-based foods has helped to uplift my mood and increase my energy levels. All those lovely vitamins I get from fresh greens and fruit help keep my body in good health.

Regardless of the diet you choose, there are a few foods and dietary changes that are sure to boost your mood. Some of them might sound obvious, but very few of us make these changes.

1. **Alcohol**

   I'm diving straight into a touchy one. Drinking a lot can take its toll on your health. Body and mind are connected so your mood and happiness can suffer too. There's nothing wrong with the occasional drink with friends if it brings you joy in the present moment but consider reducing your consumption. You *will* feel better. I don't drink anymore apart from rare occasions. So, if we meet, don't tempt me with a glass of bubbly, I won't neck it.

2. **Processed foods**

   If your grandmother wouldn't know what it is, then don't eat it. While many foods we eat are processed (bread, cheese, canned beans), the problems arise when we eat food that's been modified with too much salt, sugar, fats, preservatives or anything artificial. Try to stick with single ingredient foods that haven't been jingled with! Stay away from the artificial stuff and read the labels to monitor how much salt, sugar and fats are in ya food! I feel in a much better mood when I eat basic food, as nature intended.

3. **Too much caffeine**

I can already feel the jaw of my coffee-loving friends drop. Too much caffeine from any source, even from tea can make you feel anxious, tired and even angry! Don't worry, anything below 3 cups a day is unlikely to have an adverse effect, it's only over-consumption that's problematic. With our busy and stressful lives, many people heavily over-consume caffeine and it's impacting their happiness.

Add to Your Diet

1. **Matcha Green Tea**

Used by monks to aid meditation practices and famous for its never-ending list of health benefits, this green powder could be a real alternative to coffee for you. Before you tell me, it doesn't taste good and looks like pond water, let me tell you why it's a legendary beverage to support your happiness. Matcha has mood-boosting effects due to the amino acid L-Theanine. It makes you feel calm but alert, just like meditation. Although matcha does have caffeine, you don't get the jitteriness you get from other caffeinated drinks.

2. **More H20**

Drink more water. Our bodies are around 60% water yet most of us don't drink enough of it. Not drinking enough water can hugely impact your energy levels, overall health, and mood. Dehydration can make you feel stressed, tired and rundown. A glass of water first thing in the morning will kickstart your metabolism and boost your mood. Doctors suggest eight glasses or two litres a day. I would recommend drinking even more, especially when you exercise. Ten glasses or 2.5 litres is the sweet spot for me.

3. **Vitamin D**

Not enough Vitamin D could be making us grumpy. Naturally, we absorb vitamin D from sunlight but as we spend most of our time working indoors, we often don't get enough of it especially during the long winter months. Vitamin D is turned into a hormone in our bodies and it's hugely important for us functioning properly. It plays a crucial role in calcium absorption, supports the immune system and brain function and helps to keep our dopamine and serotonin in good shape!

Vitamin D supplements or natural sources such as cod liver oil, egg yolk, salmon and oysters can help to boost your mood. It's a good idea to get your vitamin D levels checked before you start popping supplements.

4. **Natural mood boosters**

During my illness, I experimented with some natural remedies to boost my mood and immune system. While you don't want to become reliant on these to feel good, they can be great in balancing your mood. I have found two herbs that worked amazingly for me.

- **Ashwagandha**: A plant used in traditional Indian medicine (Ayurveda) for centuries. While its name unappealingly translates to 'horse-smell', its benefits are incredible.
  Ashwagandha is an adaptogen meaning that it balances your hormones to manage your body's stress response. Life can get stressful and Ashwagandha can be our secret little helper. It helps to reduce stress, improve sleep, increase energy levels and make you feel calm. I took it during the final weeks at university and I felt it helped me ace my exams and presentations. I should order some more soon!

- **Maca Root**: Native to Peru, this is another adaptogen. It's often used to tackle chronic fatigue as it enhances energy and stamina. It's worked well for me although Ashwagandha is still my favourite. There is black, yellow and red maca. Red is supposed to be best for females and black for males. Yellow is the most commonly harvested as it's used in Peruvian cooking! Maca is also highly popular these days for improving sexual health.

It's useful to cycle the use of adaptogens. I take them for four weeks and then take a couple of months break before I take them again. To be safe, speak to your doctor before taking any especially if you have a thyroid condition.

5. **Vitamins, Minerals & Antioxidants**

Getting sufficient vitamins, minerals and antioxidants is vital for a healthy and happy life. If you eat a balanced diet, you shouldn't have to supplement but sometimes a natural supplement boost can work wonders too.

Top foods I'd recommend adding to your diet - Cashew nuts (nature's vitamin pill), brazil nuts, hemp seeds, dark chocolate, walnuts, kale, turmeric, ginger, spinach, mushrooms, blueberries.

6. **Fermented foods**

While the idea of eating fermented food might not be making you dribble right away, there are good reasons to be eating them! There's been much research in recent years demonstrating the importance of a healthy gut on your emotional and mental well-being. The 'gut-brain axis' exchanges information through neurotransmitters from your gut to the brain. That's why you might have an upset stomach when you're stressed and nervous or you might become gassy (whoops)! When you keep your gut healthy, your brain is in better health too. Fermented foods have plenty of good bacteria that help to keep your gut in check. Try adding some of the following foods into your diet - yoghurt, kombucha, sauerkraut, kimchi, nattō (this one is tough for me) or pickles.

Felix New's tip:

Try practising gratitude for the food and drink you consume. It'll make you appreciate your food more, make it taste better and make you feel better!

KEEP AN EYE ON YOUR SLEEP!

Good sleep helps to manage our emotions, immune system, recovery, energy, and mood. Poor sleep takes a toll on all of the above.

How much sleep is enough? Only you will know the answer to that. Our bodies work differently. I know some people who consistently sleep three hours a night and are perfectly lively and happy. Research has suggested that getting less than six hours a night could be damaging our health in the long run. Equally, sleeping too long will make you feel lethargic and give you less time in the day, which might make you more stressed. This means less time to be happy.

Find what works for you and try to keep your bedtime and wake-up time consistent. Your mood will improve when your body can adjust to a reasonably reliable sleep schedule.

Try not to expose yourself to blue light from electric devices at least one hour before bedtime. If we overexpose ourselves to blue light, our body's sleep-inducing melatonin production will be negatively impacted and our sleep quality will be worse. Try to meditate or practise deep breathing before sleeping to calm yourself down. You could even whack a little lavender oil on your pillow to help you relax and fall asleep quicker.

DEVELOP A MORNING ROUTINE

"The way you start your day determines how well you live your day."
Robin Sharma

The morning is a chance to have some YOU time and set yourself up for a great day. A morning routine could involve meditation, affirmation, practising gratitude, exercising, stretching, reading or praying.

Many successful people like Barack Obama, Steve Jobs and Lady Gaga attribute a large part of their success and well-being to their morning routine. When you have a morning routine, you start your day in a positive way with a clear mind and a feeling of having already accomplished something. This positivity and sense of accomplishment then carries you through your day and can significantly enhance your mood.

I would advise against checking your social media or e-mail first thing in the morning. When you scroll through your phone first thing in the morning, you take a passive attitude towards your day. Check your phone only after you've completed your morning routine. When you have a morning routine, you're *active* and not *reactive*. When you have an active state of mind, the world is yours for the taking, and your mood will change for the better.

If you have family or work commitments that don't give you time in the morning, try to get up earlier or create a bullet-proof night-time routine instead.

CUT DOWN ON SOCIAL MEDIA

Social media is not always so helpful when it comes to our happiness. Despite allowing us to share parts of our lives with friends and followers, these platforms are also designed to make us use them often. We can get hooked on the dopamine spikes when someone likes our content. Our brain rewards us with feel-good hormones but it's a false sense of accomplishment. What have you achieved by someone liking your picture?

We can get sad when comparing ourselves to other people's lives. Somehow, our own life can't seem to keep up with all those pictures and stories. I struggle with it too. When I'm using social media to post inspirational content, I'm susceptible to falling into the social media addiction trap. Research on social media addiction is in its early stages but there are links to depression, anxiety, and even suicide. We need to monitor our use carefully. We should try spending more time giving our full attention to the people in our real life.

To reduce social media use, try to check social media at set times in the day. This will reduce the compulsive checking and hunger for likes. You could even try a social media detox and stop using social media entirely for some time. Be real with yourself about your usage and how it's affecting you!

GET OUT INTO NATURE MORE!

Being in nature massively boosts your happiness. It makes you feel more present and peaceful, and the fresh air improves your health and mood. Get out into nature more often and make use of the treasure that was gifted to us.

SLOW YOUR LIFE DOWN

Are you running from deadline to deadline? Are you in constant demand on social media? Do you feel that you can never unplug from the stress and busyness of your life? Do you feel drained every day?

It might be time to slow your life down. You'll become happier as a result of hitting the breaks.

Say NO!

Say NO more often to things that will add to your stress. Realise that sometimes it's okay to let some income go and instead, trade it for time to relax or be with your loved ones. Yes, money is important and sometimes we need to work hard to pay the bills and progress in life, but what's the use if you're barely living a meaningful existence? You deserve to enjoy your life and slow things down. As a friend told me when I was caught up in the rat race, "Felix, live a little!". That was a wake-up call for me.

Set up an auto-responder on your e-mail. Say no to social media. You'll be surprised, you won't miss anything important.

> Here you can apply two tools you've discovered in this book. Acceptance & Presence. Accept that things might not always be the way they should be. Learn to be okay with saying *no* to things. Some things can wait. Allow yourself to slow your life down. You don't need to run around like a headless chicken. Enjoy the present moment with your loved ones or enjoy your own company. When your thoughts drift off to work, bring your attention back to the present moment and voilà, you have successfully slowed your life down. It's a process

and takes practise but it's highly rewarding.

Outsource More Often

Why waste hours of your valuable time doing things that someone else can do for you cheaply and probably more professionally? Build up a network of efficient and high-quality contacts who can help give you more freedom. Let other people do the tasks you hate doing. While you might hate doing laundry, someone else might like doing it. Make a list and see what you can outsource. When you're on a tight budget, it can be hard to outsource parts of your life but with some research and planning, there's often a way to make your life easier and less stressful. You could also talk to your friends and see if you can help each other do the tasks you don't enjoy doing.

Say No and Outsource more!

MAKE MORE MONEY

Hold on. Didn't you just say I should slow my life down?! Isn't my Happiness Button all about achieving internal happiness?

Hear me out. Having more money can help you live more peacefully and freely. This is not a book on becoming financially free - I'm still trying to crack that nut myself. However, you'll find that with increased happiness, you'll start to attract more wealth and opportunities naturally. *MONEY* by Rob Moore is great to understand how money works.

Here are some tips on increasing your income

- Start an eBay shop, selling things around the house you don't need
- Write a book. Sell a physical copy, e-book or audiobook
- Start your own clothing brand with no start-up costs! (e.g. Teespring.com)
- Pet sitting
- Rent out a room on Airbnb
- Distrokid.com – upload your music or spoken word and start earning!

- Review websites (e.g. UserTesting.com - $10 for 20 minutes)
- Freelance your skills online (e.g. Upwork.com, Fiverr.com)
- Drop shipping products (sell via Shopify, Amazon or eBay)
- Blogging/Affiliate Marketing (build an email list or social media following)
- YouTube Channel (monetize videos via Google AdSense)
- Instagram page (advertise others or your services)
- Learn how to invest your money (*The Intelligent Investor* by Benjamin Graham is a classic).

The internet has made it easier than ever to increase your income from home and thus potentially also increasing your freedom.

BE ACTIVE. BE A CREATOR!

It's important to create. You should create because you want to, not because you have to. It marks a key difference in your mood. Instead of eating out, cook for yourself and your loved ones. Instead of buying art, create your own pictures to hang up around the house. You can derive great happiness from creating rather than consuming. This applies to all areas of life. Be active, be a creator.

KEEP A DAILY OR WEEKLY SUCCESS LOG

Draw up a list of what you want to achieve today, or even this week. Tick off each item as you complete it.

Keeping a success log reminds you of the things you've achieved. When you don't keep a success log, your mind might be quick to scan for reasons for why you're 'a failure'. Once such thoughts pop into your mind, you simply bring up your success log and remind yourself of how great you're doing. You can even flick through past success logs if you'd like. Although it sounds fancy, a success log is essentially a to-do list that make you feel good.

They should be things that are in your control. I would write *create a high-quality video* instead of *create a video that gets many views.* I don't have control over how many views my video gets but I can focus on successfully creating a high-quality video.

USE AN OBJECT TO TRIGGER YOUR HAPPINESS

This is a genius idea from my friend Nathan's YouTube channel *A Helpful Earth.*

Step 1: Pick an object.

Step 2: Every time you see this object, recall positive things that made you feel good in the past such as relaxing on a beach or eating your favourite food. Repeat it every time you see the object. You'll start to associate positive feelings with this object.

Step 3: After a week or so, you'll no longer need to bring these positive things to mind because when you see that object, it will automatically trigger positive emotions. Simple and genius. Try it!

DO MORE OF WHAT YOU LOVE

What do you love doing? Do these activities more often. This might seem like common sense, but we often don't make enough time for what we love doing and our happiness suffers as a result. Put it in your diary. Do more of it. Make the most of this life.

IMAGINE YOU'RE 100 YEARS OLD!

Imagine you're a whopping 100 years old. You're wise but you also don't have many years left to live. What advice would you give to your current self? Probably to do more of what you love and what makes you happy, and to stop sweating the little things that annoy you.

KEEP AN EYE ON YOUR POSTURE

A hunched-up posture represents being weak, unhappy or even anxious. Not only might you feel weak with such a stance, but people might also perceive you as insecure and unhappy and treat you accordingly.

Try to straighten up your spine and keep your gaze straight ahead. An upright posture demonstrates confidence to others and yourself. When you feel more confident, you feel happier. A 2014 study in the *Journal of Behavior Therapy and Experimental Psychiatry* by Michalak and co. found that people who walked happily, thought more positively! Change your posture, change your mood.

COLD EXPOSURE

Wim Hoff, 'the Iceman', arguably made the benefits of cold exposure go viral. He climbed Mount Kilimanjaro in nothing but shorts, swam under ice for 66 meters and survived being in a container covered with nothing but ice cubes for almost two hours.

Why would anyone in their right mind do such a thing?

The cold has immense health benefits that can boost happiness. It improves metabolism, reduces inflammation, improves immune system response, and promotes better mental health.

You don't need to do these crazy things to experience the benefits. Cold showers are a start. *Cold what? But I love my hot showers.* People often hate the idea of replacing their nice warm showers with cold ones. It doesn't have to be hard. Start warm and slowly move to as cold as it gets! Do 30 seconds of cold and slowly work your way up. You will feel like a BOSS throughout your day. If you can master the cold, not much else can get in your way! In his TED talk *Cold Shower Therapy*, Joel Runyon details the immense benefits of cold showers. Joel says growth, success, and happiness is found in facing discomfort from time to time.

If you're now excited to take a cold shower, be sure to ease your way into it. You don't want to get sick. The discipline you develop in the shower will carry through to other areas of your life.

STAND UP FOR YOUR BELIEFS

If you don't stand for something, you will fall for anything

Elisha Long, an entrepreneur and Youtuber put this point into a strikingly beautiful metaphor. *Draw a line in the sand and stand up for your beliefs.*

Imagine you're on a beach with someone trying to convince you to do something you don't agree with. Draw a line in the sand. This line represents your beliefs, it's what you stand for. You will not step over the line into the other person's land of beliefs. This is your land and you will stay there if you please. Of course, sometimes it's necessary to re-draw your line but don't re-draw it to please others.

Life's too short to try and please others all the time. Do what you believe in. It's hard to stand up for your own beliefs when people disagree with you, test you, or hate on you for not doing what *they* want you to do but that's okay. Standing up for your beliefs gives you a great sense of self-control and happiness. You are the captain of your ship. If you don't stand for something, you will fall for anything. You're doing a great job at navigating your ship. Keep it up!

SUMMARY OF STEPS

1. Be Mindful of Who You Spend Time With
2. Don't Forget the Mind-Body Connection
3. Keep an Eye on Your Sleep!
4. Develop a Morning Routine
5. Cut Down on Social Media
6. Get out Into Nature More
7. Slow Your Life Down
8. Make More Money
9. Be Active. Be A Creator!
10. Keep a Daily or Weekly Success Log

11. Use an Object to Trigger Your Happiness

12. Do More of What You Love

13. Imagine You're 100 Years Old!

14. Keep an Eye on Your Posture

15. Cold Exposure

16. Stand Up for Your Beliefs

Since this is *your* guide to developing happiness, use the blank space below to add any steps that help you amplify your happiness and support your Happiness Button. You can then remind yourself of them at any time.

Like the fairy tale Hansel and Gretel, I like to leave breadcrumbs when I find something that works for me, so I can find my way back to it. If something is working for me, I'll write it down.

_____

_____

_____

_____

INSPIRATIONAL PEOPLE TO FOLLOW ONLINE

Many of these people have inspired this book and are friends of mine. They act as guides and mentors in my life. Sometimes, I like to listen to their videos almost like mini audiobooks. Your list will be different but here are some people that resonate with me and I think could be useful resources for you.

Prince Ea, Preston Smiles, Alexi Panos, Olly Sheehan, Frankie Cote, Tony Shavers III, David Goggins, Thomas Bilyeu, Donald Arteaga, Matt D'Avella, Improvement Pill, Eric Ho, Actualized.org (Leo),

Dan Lok, Burnell Washburn, Nick Vujicic, Luke Truth, aanghel, The Five Elements (Diana), Happy Facts Lifestyle, A Helpful Earth, Noah Elkrief, Mike Vestil, Jane Fey, Ty Speaks, Modern Health Monk (Alexander Heyne), Seth Alexander, Vishen Lakhiani, Wendi Blum, Felix New (this guy is a must follow), Tim Ferris, Jay Shetty, TheUnconditionalTruth, Elisha Long, Kieferfreund, Authentic Self Guide, WakeUpFulfilled.com (Gavin Stephenson) and of course, the one and only Eckhart Tolle.

Additional Resources

Morning Routines: An excellent book on morning routines is *The Miracle Morning: The Not-So-Obvious Secret Guaranteed to Transform Your Life (Before 8AM)* by Hal Elrod. The author himself gets up at around 4am each day!

CONCLUSION

It's one of my aims for this book and my time here on earth to make it cool to openly seek true happiness. To make it cool to be present in the moment. To make it cool to meditate. To make it cool to practise acceptance. To make it cool to be grateful for what you have. To make it cool to practise positive self-talk and affirmations. To make it cool to be compassionate to others and yourself. To make it cool to enjoy your journey and embrace change. To make it bad-ass to face your emotions and fears. To make true happiness accessible to all.

We need to seriously move away from the idea that seeking happiness is something for 'alternative' people. While self-help techniques are not the solution to everything, many people are suffering the effects of an unhappy existence because self-help tools are labelled as 'hippy'. Living a hedonistic lifestyle and only seeking pleasure in the form of materialism or focusing on the final destination far too much hasn't done us much good. We are just not happy following this path. We need a cultural and global shift in the way we approach happiness as individuals, as nations, and as the world as a whole.

There have been some positive movements in this direction with more people 'waking up', but we still have far to go. Almost half the world's population has an internet connection but how many people in the world experience true happiness? Unfortunately, I think we have way more internet users than happy people (and many very unhappy internet users).

If the things you've discovered in this book have been helpful, I would urge you to share them with your friends and anyone you meet. Why not spark up a conversation about happiness? You don't need to tell everyone to buy my book (although if you do, that's appreciated!). All I ask is that you spread the positivity and insights you have gained from *My Happiness Button*. Maybe you can be part of driving true happiness forward.

Being happy doesn't mean always feeling happy.

As you go through life working on your happiness, it's okay to feel down sometimes. It's part of your existence, and you shouldn't deny yourself of it. This world is beautiful, so get out there and experience it. It's a great time to be alive. Take good care of your Happiness Button.

Dear people of the world, we have work to do. We all need to develop our Happiness Button and activate it!

It's now up to you to use and share all you've discovered. Be part of the 10% who take action. You deserve to be happy. We all do.

Much love,

Felix

MY HAPPINESS BUTTON CHALLENGE

I want you to become happier as a result of reading this book. However, I also know how hard it is to implement new things in our lives. Life gets busy and overwhelming and before we know it, we've forgotten most of what we read even if the information could have improved our life tremendously.

So, I came up with the idea of a challenge to keep you committed to what you discover in this book. This is to get the ball rolling and support you in developing more happiness in your life. I present to you the 30-day *My Happiness Button Challenge.*

#MyHappinessButtonChallenge

Let's Get Started!

The challenge is designed to give you a taster of each chapter in the book. It allows you to dip your toes into each topic and avoids exposing you to too much new information at once. It should be enjoyable and a little challenging but not overwhelming. It's never a good idea to try and do too much at once. You might end up not doing anything and your mind might reject it all. That's why the challenge is separated into bitesize and manageable steps. We will focus on two topics a week for the next 30 days.

Every day, review the 'Steps to Happiness via...' section in each chapter for the two topics of the week. Choose to apply at least one step for each topic. As you go through the challenge, you can keep up any steps from previous weeks but also leave space to engage with the new topics.

The breakdown of the topics and weeks is as follows:

Days 1 - 7 (Week 1)
Presence & Acceptance

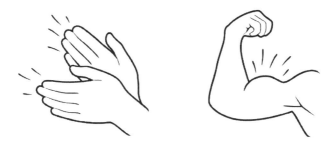

Days 7 - 14 (Week 2)
Gratitude & Affirmations

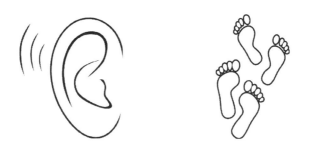

Days 14 - 21 (Week 3)
Compassion & Enjoying the Journey/Embracing Change

Days 21 - 30 (Week 4)
Facing Fears/Negative Emotions &
Additional Happiness Boosters

What Resources are Available to Support Me?

I'm providing a bunch of free resources you can download from Felixnew.com and I'll be available on the Facebook group *MyHappinessButton Group* to guide you during the challenge. In the group, you can update us about your progress and interact with other people building up their Happiness Button. We're building a friendly and supportive community there. Get your friends involved!

I have a *free tracker* available at Felixnew.com where you can hold yourself accountable during the challenge by ticking off your progress. I'm also only an e-mail away.

Are You Allowed to Cheat?

If there's something in the book you're keen to try, you can do it at any time. Don't let the challenge restrict you. It's just here as a rough guide to channel your focus. If you want to practise your compassion and buy someone a coffee during week one then feel free to do so. This is *your* Happiness Button and you're the captain of your ship in this ocean of life. You can't really cheat, only if you're being lazy with the steps. Then you're cheating yourself.

What Happens After The 30-day Challenge?

Once you've completed the challenge, start reviewing the chapters again in your own time. I encourage you to keep up any exercises and steps you enjoyed during the 30-day challenge. If they resonate with you, they are likely to bring your results. Taking the time to dive a little deeper into each chapter and topic could also be a good idea for the future.

What If I Don't Want to Do the Challenge?

Don't worry I won't leave you out in the cold, you're also part of the pack.

Are You Ready?

I look forward to hearing about your challenge and experience with this book. Everyone tends to structure it a little differently! Use the hashtag #MyHappinessButtonChallenge to spread awareness on social media. You can also tag me in your posts, although I'm working on spending less time on social media, so I'll try my best to respond. You can always drop me an e-mail to tell me about your progress - I'd love to hear how you're getting on.

Get in Touch with Me

Website

www.felixnew.com

Email

info@felixnew.com

Social Media

Instagram: @thefelixnew

Facebook & YouTube: Felix New

Notes
Chapter 1

Study on Happiness and Depression Genes
Okbay, A., Baselmans, B., De Neve, J., Turley, P., Nivard, M., Fontana, M., ... & Gratten, J. (2016). Genetic variants associated with subjective well-being, depressive symptoms, and neuroticism identified through genome-wide analyses. *Nature genetics*.

Money and Happiness Link Study
Kahneman, D., & Deaton, A. (2010). High income improves evaluation of life but not emotional well-being. *Proceedings of the national academy of sciences*.

Happiness Studies on Life Expectancy
Chei, C. L., Lee, J. M. L., Ma, S., & Malhotra, R. (2018). Happy older people live longer. *Age and Ageing*.
Liu, B., Floud, S., Pirie, K., Green, J., Peto, R., Beral, V., & Million Women Study Collaborators. (2016). Does happiness itself directly affect mortality? The prospective UK Million Women Study. *The Lancet*.

ONS UK Happiness Levels Rising?
https://www.ons.gov.uk/peoplepopulationandcommunity/well-being/bulletins/measuringnationalwell-being/april2017tomarch2018

Jobs at Risk Due to Automation
https://www.pwc.co.uk/services/economics-policy/insights/the-impact-of-automation-on-jobs.html

Depression Stats
https://www.who.int/news-room/fact-sheets/detail/depression
https://www.bcbs.com/the-health-of-america/reports/major-depression-the-impact-overall-health

Jam Experiment
Iyengar, S. S., & Lepper, M. R. (2000). When choice is demotivating: Can one desire too much of a good thing? *Journal of personality and social psychology*.

Chapter 3

Survey on Number of Meditators
https://mindworks.org/blog/how-many-people-meditate/

How Meditation Can Change Your Brain
https://www.expandinglight.org/blog/meditation/meditation-teacher-training/how-meditation-changes-your-brain/
https://mindworks.org/blog/how-meditation-changes-the-brain/

Benefits of Meditation
Reduced Stress
Chin, B., Slutsky, J., Raye, J., & Creswell, J. (2018). Mindfulness Training Reduces Stress at Work: a Randomized Controlled Trial. *Mindfulness.*

Further Benefits
https://www.scienceofpeople.com/meditation-benefits/

Chapter 4

Link Between Happiness and Disease
Angner, E., Ghandhi, J., Purvis, K., Amante, D., & Allison, J. (2013). Daily functioning, health status, and happiness in older adults. *Journal of Happiness Studies*, *14*(5), 1563-1574.

Chapter 5

Gratitude to Boost Immune system
https://www.wellmune.com/2017/11/21/10542/

Chapter 6

Donut Scanner Study on Affirmations
Cascio, C., O'Donnell, M., Tinney, F., Lieberman, M., Taylor, S., Strecher, V., & Falk, E. (2015). Self-affirmation activates brain systems associated with self-related processing and reward and is reinforced by future orientation. *Social Cognitive and Affective Neuroscience.*

Chapter 7

Aravind the Compassionate Eye Hospital
https://opinionator.blogs.nytimes.com/2013/01/16/in-india-leading-a-hospital-franchise-with-vision/

Spending Money on Others Makes Us Happier
https://hbr.org/2013/06/how-money-actually-buys-happiness

Chapter 9

Negative Effects of Suppressing Emotions
Gross, J. & Levenson, R. (1997). Hiding feelings: the acute effects of inhibiting negative and positive emotion. *Journal of abnormal psychology.* See more from leading expert James Gross on emotions: https://spl.stanford.edu/james-gross-phd-0

Deep Breathing Decreased PTSD in Veterans
Seppälä, E., Nitschke, J., Tudorascu, D., Hayes, A., Goldstein, M., Nguyen, D., ... & Davidson, R. (2014). Breathing-based meditation decreases posttraumatic stress disorder symptoms in US Military veterans: A randomized controlled longitudinal study. *Journal of traumatic stress.*

Chapter 10

The Importance of Close Social Relationships for Happiness
https://www.adultdevelopmentstudy.org/

UK Loneliness Study
Red Cross & Co-op Report on Loneliness: Trapped in a bubble https://www.redcross.org.uk/get-involved/partner-with-us/our-partners/co-op

Behavioural Science Study on Posture and Happiness
Michalak, J., Rohde, K., & Troje, N. F. (2015). How we walk affects what we remember: Gait modifications through biofeedback change negative affective memory bias. *Journal of Behavior Therapy and Experimental Psychiatry.*

Cold Exposure – Benefits
https://www.wimhofmethod.com/benefits

39183081R00115

Printed in Poland
by Amazon Fulfillment
Poland Sp. z o.o., Wrocław